A Guide
to the Plants
of the Pinnacles

by

Ralph C. Webb

September

1971

Published by the Southwest Parks & Monuments
Association in cooperation with the National
Park Service and Pinnacles National Monument

Copyright September 1971

Library of Congress Catalog Card No. 72—172690

Standard Book No. 0-911408-25-8

i

ACKNOWLEDGEMENT

A need for this publication existed when I first arrived at Pinnacles because the spring wildflower show is so diverse and lavish it is almost impossible to keep up with it and provide those who are interested with the information they desire about the flowers and other plants that grow here. I decided to try putting something together to fill this need but I wasn't too sure I could do it. Thanks to the many seasonal staff members who assisted me and the forebearance of Gordon Patterson, the superintendent, we have managed to get the job done. I am indebted to Earl Jackson, Executive director of the Southwest Parks & Monuments Association, for his aid and encouragement toward getting this published and to Charles T. Mason, Jr., Curator of the University of Arizona Herbarium, for checking the manuscript and making many helpful suggestions and comments.

INTRODUCTION

Plants are like people; you seldom ever find them alone. They nearly always occur in definite communities which can be easily recognized, if you know what to look for. Humans live in agricultural, industrial, retirement, and other types of communities. Each type is determined by the kind of people living in it, climate, geography, and other factors. So it is with plants. They also form communities composed of species which almost always seem to occur together. The kind of plant community that will grow in a given place is affected by the same climate, soil, geography, and other factors that affect the human communities.

Here at Pinnacles we are fortunate to have only four kinds of plant communities to learn. Each is distinct from the others and easy to recognize. This is often not so elsewhere. Plant communities frequently blend with one another so gradually it is difficult to tell where one starts and the other stops; a problem shared by human communities along both coasts of the United States. Once you have learned what to look for here, you should have little trouble recognizing each community. We could go into greater detail but it isn't necessary. All we wish to do is make it easier for you to know what kind of plant or flower you are looking at. Don't be discouraged if you can't score 100%; botanists can't either.

We have not included all the plants of the monument for several reasons. We have no good record of the mosses and liverworts or lichens and I am not qualified to properly identify them. As a result, these have been left out. It is quite likely we have overlooked some plants entirely. It is also likely we have made a few mistakes. If so, we would appreciate your calling them to our attention. The scientific names are all based on "A California Flora" by MUNZ. All the plants are recorded in our herbarium or the photo-file.

This small book started as a checklist of the plants at Pinnacles. In order to answer questions of the many serious amateurs visiting here, I decided to add a little here — a little there — a little somewhere else. As a result, I no longer had a simple checklist; it had become something else. I'm not sure what, but I call it "A Guide to the Plants of Pinnacles." I hope those of you who are interested, but have no botany background, will find this publication both useable and useful.

Ralph C. Webb

1

THE PLANT COMMUNITIES

The communities you know might be called San Jose, Salinas, or Hollister. The four plant communities here at Pinnacles are called the Xeric (zee-rick), Riparian (rye-pear-ee-an), Chaparral (Shap-par-el) and Foothill Woodland. Their place on the hills or in the valleys, the rock from which their soil was derived, the amount of sun they get, and many other things determine which will be which and where you will find them. Each is described below with some of the more important reasons for their being the way they are included in the description.

XERIC

This community is best described as the bare-rock community. It is found on exposed cliff faces and rocky out-crops which possess little or no soil. The main plants of this community are lichens, mosses, spike mosses, and succulents such as live-forevers and dudleyas. I have not included the lichens and mosses for the reasons stated in the introduction. In this community water is scarce, little soil accumulates, and the temperatures are extreme. Any plant capable of living here must be very tough and adaptable. There may be pockets of soil, here and there, where you will find grasses and flowers from other communities. They are merely islands in the Xeric community, not a regular part of it.

RIPARIAN

The Riparian community is most noticeable in early spring when winter rains have deposited a copious supply of moisture to its account. This is the community of water loving plants; plants needing abundant water to survive. You will find it centered around the springs and streambeds. Cat-tails, ferns, duckweed, blackberries, willows, cottonwoods, and sycamores are some of the most common plants found here. "Just a minute!" you object. "I've been here in the summer and there hasn't been any water in the streambeds where the cottonwoods and willows were growing. They were bone-dry!" You would be partly correct in your objection. During the hot summer months most of the streambeds are dry along much of their length with only a few pockets of water occuring here and there. If you were to dig 1½ to 2 feet under the surface, however, you would find an underground flow of water which exists year-round. A Riparian community must have an abundant year-around source of water available, but not necessarily visible. Most of the major drainage channels at Pinnacles have flowing underground streams in their channels the entire year. The plants will show you where the water is.

XERIC COMMUNITY

RIPARIAN COMMUNITY

CHAPARRAL COMMUNITY

FOOTHILL WOODLAND COMMUNITY

5

── CHAPARRAL ──

The meaning of the word "chaparral" is often misunderstood and many have the impression it means a single kind of plant. Chaparral is a plant community, like the preceding two, but one that covers about 80% of the entire monument. It is one of the most important features of the Pinnacles. No other National Park area has such an extensive or truly representative stand of coast-range chaparral. As the Xeric covers the ridgetops, and the Riparian covers the stream bottoms, the Chaparral covers all but a small portion of the hillsides. It is the dense brushy cover of the hills. When you look closely you can see a pronounced difference between the chaparral communities on the north and south facing slopes of the hills. About 90% of the vegetation on the south facing slopes is chamise, a dry needle-leaved plant with brittle branches. Other plants do occur but only in small scattered patches; mainly buck-brush and manzanita. The same three plants occur on the north facing slopes but the amount of chamise decreases considerably and there is an abundance of holly-leaf cherry and toyon. This change of plant distri-bution causes the north slopes to have a darker more lush-green color. We call these two kinds moist-phase and dry-phase chaparral. There are several reason for the difference between the moist-phase and dry-phase chapparral communities. The north slopes receive less sunlight during the year and are therefore cooler. The cooler temperature allows more moisture to be retained over a longer period of time, more types of plants to become established, and a more dense plant population which causes more humus to develop in the soil which then can hold more water. The south slopes, having more sunlight, are hotter and drier. Only the hardiest of plants are able to get a foothold here and become established. Neither of the two types of chaparral grow in an easy environment. All the plants of the chaparral, moist or dry-phase, must be adapted to surviving long periods of heat and drought. Its soil, at best, is coarse and gravelly. Even the soil of the moist-phase areas will hold water only a short time and the plants must either grow and produce seed before the winter moisture disappears or have a way to store or get water during the hot dry part of the year. The dense shrubbery of the chaparral provides a haven for an amazing number of different wildlife species.

── FOOTHILL WOODLAND ──

The foothill woodland community is the only other community on the hillsides. It also occupies some hilltops. Though it covers only 7% of the monument, it is just as important as the chaparral. It is easily recog-nized as those areas covered by grasses dotted with blue oak and digger pine. The soil of this community is much finer than that of the chapar-ral and also much richer in organic material. Its one draw-back is its shallow depth; 2 feet or less. Because of this, it is incapable of holding water for any great length of time. The plants growing here either undergo their entire life cycle, from sprout to seed, during the wet spring months or they have roots which reach a permanent source of water, like the blue oak and digger pine which send their roots as much as 150 feet down to a permanent source of water. Though this community covers only a small area, it supplies as much as 70% of the monument wildlife's food. It is the Pinnacles bread-basket.

Now that you know a little more about plant communities, I think you will find the plant list a little easier to use than it might seem at first glance. It's all a matter of being aware of your environment. If you know what to expect in each community, what time of year to expect it, about how the plant looks, and the flower color of those plants with flowers, you should be able to identify far more plants than you ever thought you could. If you learn how to use the simple key to the families you should have no more than a dozen plants to choose from and with the other clues things should go quite well. It might not be the easiest thing you have ever done but I imagine you will find a great deal of satisfaction in doing it yourself.

Don't try eating any plant until you are absolutely certain of the plant being what you think it is and that you know how to properly prepare it for internal consumption!

•

Collecting plants in the monument cannot be done without a permit and a valid educational research project.

•

HELP US PRESERVE OUR PLANTS; DON'T PICK THE FLOWERS!

SUGGESTED REFERENCES

Most of the information was taken from "A California Flora" by P. A. Munz and the "Manual of the Flowering Plants of California" by W. L. Jepson. The ethnobotany was garnered from diverse sources. Many natural history and conservation publications contain good sources of ethnobotany, or plant uses, in their stories on primitive cultures and folkways. Many survival handbooks are also good sources of information.

HOW TO USE THE BOOK

The key to the families is divided into 2 parts; those plants without flower or seed and those with flowers and/or seeds. In these 2 sections an "either/or" choice key is used. As an example you would get to the morning-glory family by making the choices illustrated below:

PLANTS WITH FLOWERS AND/OR SEEDS

FLOWERING PLANTS

PLANTS WITH NET-VEINED LEAVES, FLOWER PARTS IN 5'S
(DICOTS)

(DICOTS)

PETALS PRESENT AND EVIDENT

FLOWER PETALS FUSED TOGETHER . . . .(GROUP V)
(GROUP V)

OVARY ENCLOSED IN OR ABOVE THE FLOWER

STAMENS 5 OR LESS

PLANTS GREEN: NOT PARASITES

FLOWERS REGULAR

1 PISTIL

STAMENS LESS THAN PETAL LENGTH

FLOWERS NOT AS ABOVE

OVARY HAS 3 OR FEWER PARTS

STYLE TIP NOT 3 PARTED

5 DISTINCT SEPALS

VINE-LIKE PLANTS (MORNING-GLORY
FAMILY) PAGE 32

The choices above are those you would need to make from each pair of choices to describe a plant of the morning-glory family. No other family in the key fits this exact description. After you decide which family your plant belongs to, turn to that family in the book. Except for the sunflower family, you will then have no more than a dozen plants to choose from. Each plant is described as shown below:

(common name)   (scientific name)   (flower color, or shape, if
                                          flower is present)

☐ WIND POPPY . . . . ORANGE-RED
   Stylomecon heterophylla . . . . April-May

                FOOTHILL WOODLAND

(plant community where it is found)   (date it blooms or how
                                             long it grows)

A brief description of the plant and it uses, if known.

KEY TO THE FAMILIES

PLANTS WITHOUT FLOWERS OR SEEDS

Rush-like hollow & jointed
stems with cone-shaped
spore-bearing tips

*Horsetail
Family
Page 20*

Stems not jointed or rush-like

Low coarse moss-like plants
with awl-shaped leaves

*Spike-
Moss
Family
Page 20*

Plants with well developed
stemmed leaves, some of which
bear spore cases on their
undersides

*Fern
Family
Page 20*

PLANTS WITH FLOWERS AND/OR SEEDS

Non-flowering plants

Trees with needles and cones

*Pine
Family
Page 22*

9

Trees or shrubs with scale-like
leaves & fleshy berry-like fruit

*Juniper
Family
Page 22*

Flowering plants

    Plants with mostly broad
feather-veined or net-
veined leaves and flower
parts in 4's or 5's; rarely
in 3's

*Dicots
Page 22*

PALMATE
LOBED LEAF

    Plants with long narrow
and/or parallel veined
leaves. Flower parts in
3's; rarely 2's, 4's, or 5's

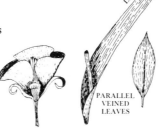

LINEAR LEAF

*Monocots
Page 63*

PARALLEL
VEINED
LEAVES

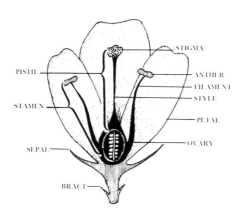

STIGMA

PISTIL

ANTHER

FILAMENT

STYLE

STAMEN

PETAL

OVARY

SEPAL

BRACT

(DICOTS)

Petals lacking (sometimes simulated by sepals)

    Woody plants (trees, shrubs & vines) . . . . *Group I*

    Non-woody plants (herbaceous,
    sometimes woody at the base) . . . . *Group II*

Petals present and evident

  Flower with distinct separate petals (some look this way but aren't)

    Stamens more than 2 times the number of petals . . . . *Group III*

    Stamens 2 times the number of petals or less . . . . . *Group IV*

  Flower petals fused together
  (sometimes only at their bases) . . . . *Group V*

(GROUP I)

The leaf divided into
separate leaflets (compound)

PALMATELY COMPOUND LEAF

PINNATELY COMPOUND LEAF

Buttercup Family
Woody vines . . . . *Page 22*

Walnut Family
Trees with 15-19 pinnate leaflets . . . . *Page 48*

The leaf not divided into leaflets (simple)

BROAD OR
NET-VEINED
LEAVES

Mistletoe Family
Plants parasitic on other plants . . . . *Page 51*

11

Plants growing normally on the ground

Trees

Flowers in catkins

Lobed or spiny-edged leaves . . . .

Oak Family
Page 47

Triangular or linear-shaped leaves . . . . .

Willow Family
Page 48

Flowers not in catkins. Large palmately lobed leaves

PALMATE
LOBED LEAF

Sycamore Family
Page 47

Shrubs

Linear leaves

Buckwheat Family
Page 28

Non-linear leaves

Alternate
Leaves

Opposite
Leaves

Alternate leaves with spiny edges . . . . .

Buckthorn Family
Page 50

Opposite leaves . . . .

Olive Family
Page 31

(GROUP II)

No petals or sepals on the flowers . . . .

Spurge Family
Page 24

Sepals present, often petal-like

More than one pistil . . . .
Buttercup Family
Page 22

One pistil only

Style & stigma single . . . .
Nettle Family
Page 48

Style & stigma divided . . . .
Buckwheat Family
Page 28

(GROUP III)

Shrubs or trees

Ear-like projections at the
bottom of the leaf-stem . . . .
Rose Family
Page 43

Not like the above, no ear-like projections . . .
Poppy Family
Page 25

Non-woody plants, except sometimes at the base

2 sepals

Plants fleshy or succulent . . . .
Moss Rose Family
Portulaca Family
Page 27

Plants not fleshy, sepals
falling when plant blooms . . . .
Poppy Family
Page 25

More than 2 sepals

Stamen filaments fused into
a tube around the pistil . . . .
Mallow Family
Page 23

Stamens distinct and numerous

Foliage surfaces rough
& prickly to the touch . . . .
Loasa Family
Page 24

Foliage surfaces not rough & prickly . . . .
Buttercup Family
Page 22

13

(GROUP IV)

Plants climbing by means of tendrils . . . .
Squash Family
Page 55

Plants not climbing

  2-5 styles that are separate to their bases

    Woody shrubs or trees

      Leaves divided into 3 leaflets . . . .
Sumac Family
Page 51

      Leaves not divided, entire

        Long narrow spiny-edged leaf . . . . . .
Rose Family
Page 43

        Leaves palmately lobed at the tip

Gooseberry Family
Saxifrage Family
Page 42

    Plants not woody (herbaceous)

      Foliage fleshy or succulent . . . .
Moss Rose Family
Portulaca Family
Page 27

      Foliage not fleshy or succulent

        Flowers borne in umbels

UMBELS

Carrot Family
Page 52

        Flowers not borne in umbels

          Leaves all at the base . . . .
Gooseberry Family
Saxifrage Family
Page 42

          Leaves not all at the base . . . . . .
Pink Family
Page 27

  1 style, sometimes divided at the tip

    Woody shrubs or trees

      Ovary below the flower . . . .
Dogwood Family
Page 53

14

Ovary enclosed in or above the flower

Irregular flowers, petals not all alike

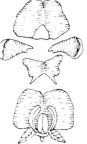

Flower resembling
a sweet-pea

Pea Family
Page 45

Flower not as above . . . .

Buckeye Family
Page 51

Regular flowers, petals all alike

LEAFLET

Compound leaves,
2-petaled flowers

Olive Family
Page 31

PINNATELY
COMPOUND
LEAF

Leaves simple & small

Wedge-shaped leaves

Buckthorn Family
Page 50

Needle-like leaves

Rose Family
Page 43

Non-woody plants, herbaceous

2 sepals; shed when flowers bloom . . . . .

Fumitory Family
Page 25

4 or more sepals

4 petals with 4 long & 2 short stamens . . .

Mustard Family
Page 25

Not as above

Regular flowers, petals alike . . . . . .

Geranium Family
Page 24

Irregular flowers, petals unlike

Pea-like flowers

Pea Family
Page 45

Flowers not pea-like . . . .

Violet Family
Page 24

(GROUP V)

Ovary enclosed in or above the flower

Stamens more than 5

Flower petals fused together
less than ½-way up . . . .

Stonecrop Family
Page 42

Flowers urn-shaped,
petals fused all the way

Heath Family
Page 30

Stamens 5 or less

Plants not green; parasites

Thin reddish wiry vine
on buckwheat bushes . . . .

Dodder Family
Page 32

Root parasites with a 2-lipped flower . . . .

Broomrape Family
Page 40

Plants not parasites, or not completely so, and green

Flowers regular, petals all alike

2 pistils with their
styles and/or
stigmas fused into
a 5-lobed unit

PISTILS

Milkweed Family
Page 31

16

1 pistil

Stamens equal to petal length and
in front or each petal . . . .

Primrose Family
Page 30

Stamens equal to or less than petal
length and alternate with petals

Small whitish dry flowers . . . . . .

Plantain Family
Page 30

Flowers not as above

Ovary in
4 parts

4 PART OVARY

Forget-me-Not
Family
Page 36

Ovary in 3 or fewer parts

Style tip 3-parted . . . .

Phlox Family
Page 32

Style tip not 3-parted

Sepals fused with
4-5 lobes showing

2 stigmas . . . .

Gentian Family
Page 31

1 stigma . . . .

Nightshade Family
Page 37

5 distinct sepals; 1-2 styles

Vine-like . . . .

Morning-Glory Family
Page 32

Prostrate, not vine-like . . .

Waterleaf Family
Page 34

Flowers irregular,
petals not all alike

Square stem cross-section . . . .

Mint Family
Page 40

Round stem cross-section . . . .

Snapdragon Family
Figwort Family
Page 37

Ovary below the flower

Stamens distinct

Leaves alternate,
flowers regular

Bellflower Family
Page 55

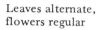

ALTERNATE
LEAVES

Leaves opposite,
flowers variable

OPPOSITE
LEAVES

Woody shrubs or vines . . . .
Honeysuckle Family
Page 54

Non-woody plants . . . .
Madder Family
Page 53

Stamens fused at their anthers

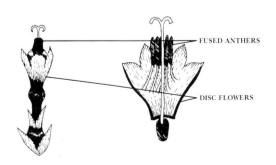

FUSED ANTHERS

Sunflower Family
Page 55

DISC FLOWERS

18

(MONOCOTS)

Flower parts reduced to bristles or scales, not petal-like

Flowers occur in the axils of chaffy scales, more or less concealed by them, with stamens and pistils protruding.

Leaf-sheaths split along
hollow stems on the side   *Grass Family*
opposite the leaf-blade . . . . *Page 67*

Leaf-sheaths encircle the
solid stem, which is   *Sedge Family*
usually 3-angled.   . . . . *Page 66*

Flowers not in the axils of
chaffy scales, not concealed

Flowers borne in dense   *Cat-Tail Family*
elongate velvety spikes . . . . *Page 64*

Flowers borne in spiky   *Rush Family*
looking globular heads . . . . *Page 65*

Flowers well developed with petal-like parts
                                             Agave Family
Woody plants with long stiff sword-like leaves . . *Page 64*

Non-woody plants, herbaceous

Flowers single, or in umbels,   *Amaryllis Family*
under which lies a papery bract . . . . *Page 64*

Flowers not in umbels, no   *Lily Family*
papery bract under them . . . . *Page 63*

NON-FLOWERING
SPORE BEARING
PLANTS

(SPIKEMOSSES)
☐ **SPIKEMOSS or LITTLE CLUBMOSS** . . . . **XERIC**
Selaginella Bigelovii
A low leafy moss-like plant standing 2 to 8 inches high and growing on thin gravelly soil in rocky areas. It is not a true moss but when it covers large areas of seemingly bare rock, it resembles moss from a distance. A close look will show it is much coarser than true moss. In the summer it has a dried up look but will quickly turn green when water is poured on it.

(HORSETAILS)
☐ **SCOURING RUSH or HORSETAIL** . . . . **RIPARIAN**
Equisetum arvense
Primitive rush-like plants with hollow stems that are solid at the joints, which are encircled by needle-like leaves. At the stem ends are cone-like spore-bearing structures. The young heads are sometimes boiled or mixed with flour and fried; the stems provide a diuretic and the grit of the outer stem layers caused them to be used for polishing ivory, brass, hardwood, and scouring pots and pans.

(FERNS)
☐ **BRACKEN FERN** . . . . **RIPARIAN**
Pteridium aquilinum
Knee-to waist-high ferns whose leaves grow on tall stalks. The leaves are as broad as they are wide and grow parallel to the ground in wet places but are quite drought resistant. Its astringency is so great it is used to tan chamois hides. It is also used as a worm medicine, diuretic, and food.

☐ **BIRD'S FOOT FERN or CLIFFBRAKE** . . . **CHAPARRAL AND
FOOTHILL WOODLAND**
Pellaea mucronata
Plants 7 to 12 inches high with wiry brown stalks and bluish-gray leaves which are divided *bipinnately*. The lower leaflets occur in clusters of three at right angles to one another. This causes them to resemble a bird's footprint. The under-rolled leaf edges cover the spore cases which occur on the underside of the leaf. They grow in hot rocky places, are very drought resistant, and often appear dead and dried up in the summer months. They rapidly come to life with the first winter rains.

☐ **COFFEE FERN or CLIFFBRAKE** . . **CHAPARRAL & RIPARIAN**
Pellaea andromedaefolia
The undercurled edges of this plant's leaves resemble grains of coffee. The leaf blades are 4 to 16 inches long, *tripinnate*, dull reddish-green to purplish above, and pale yellowish-green below. Its spore cases are similar to those of the Bird's Foot Fern.

20

☐ **GOLDBACK FERN** . . . . **RIPARIAN**
Pityrogramma triangularis
Plants 10 to 12 inches high with shiny black stalks and triangular to irregular pentagon-shaped leaves about 2 inches in length and breadth. The leaves are *tripinnate*, green on top and chartreuse to yellowish-gold below. The spore cases tend to impart a fuzzy brownish cast to the underside of the leaves. It grows in damp rock crevices.

☐ **CALIFORNIA MAIDENHAIR FERN   CHAPARRAL & RIPARIAN**
Adiantum Jordani
A beautifully delicate fern with shiny black or purplish leafstalks. The fan-shaped *pinnules* of the compound leaves are green and bear spore cases on the underside along the edges of each pinnule.

☐ **SHIELD FERN or WOOD FERN** . . . . **RIPARIAN AND
FOOTHILL WOODLAND**
Dryopteris arguta
A medium-sized fern growing in the shade with 1 to 1½ foot leaf blades which are thin and membranous, stand erect, are oblong in shape, and usually *bipinnate*. The round spore cases are borne in two parallel rows on the underside of the leaflets. A brew of these leaves was once applied locally to relieve pain and reduce discoloration of bruises, as well as taken internally to relieve depression, asthma, and dropsy.

☐ **CHAIN FERN** . . . . **RIPARIAN**
Woodwardia fimbriata
The largest fern growing here; it has 4 to 6 foot leaves which stand erect and tend to form circular stands on moist rich soil. The oblong leaf blades are *bipinnate* and its spores are borne on the underside of the leaves in recessed cavities arranged in chain-like rows; hence the name. Its tender young fiddleheads were eaten as a vegetable by the Indians.

☐ **LICORICE FERN** . . . . . . **CHAPARRAL AND RIPARIAN**
Polypodium glycyrrhiza
A medium-sized fern with 6 to 15 inch leaf blades once pinnate almost to the midrib. It is *epiphytic* and grows on rocks, tree trunks, logs, etc. The leaves die back in the summer.

FLOWERING AND/OR
SEED BEARING
PLANTS

NON-FLOWERING
PLANTS

(CONIFERS)

☑ **DIGGER PINE** . . . . **FOOTHILL WOODLAND**
Pinus sabiniana
A pine with 7 to 13 inch needles in clusters of three. The top branches are often parted into erect clusters giving its top a broom-like appearance. The cones measure as much as 7 inches in diameter by 10 inches in length and may weigh over 3 pounds. Its blue-gray foliage is not very dense, which you can prove to yourself by standing under a tree next to the trunk and looking upward through the foliage all the way to the top. The tree is named for the Digger Indians who used its large seeds for food. It is sometimes found in the Chaparral community because the natural wildfires that would normally eliminate it from that area have been suppressed over the past 80 years.

☐ **UTAH JUNIPER** . . . . **CHAPARRAL (SOMETIMES FOOTHILL WOODLAND)**

Juniperus osteosperma
A shrub or tree with sharp-pointed scale-like leaves. A close inspection will show you the sharp-pointed leaves are arranged in flattened whorls of 3. The fleshy reddish-brown fruit is not a berry but a cone with fleshy scales fused together. In some parts of the world people ferment juniper fruit with sugar and distill the result to obtain gin. Its hard round seeds are used by the Indians as beads.

FLOWERING
PLANTS

DICOTS

BUTTERCUP FAMILY
☑ **LARKSPUR** . . . . **BLUE**
Delphinium decorum   March-May

CHAPARRAL AND
FOOTHILL WOODLAND
A perennial herb with spikes of flowers appearing in the spring on grassy slopes. Sometimes known as lace weed, it has an alkaloid in its foliage which is poisonous to man and beast. Indians derived a dye from the flowers.

22

☑ **LARKSPUR** . . . . **PURPLE**
   Delphinium Parryi   April-May
CHAPARRAL AND
FOOTHILL WOODLAND
Much like the above species but the flowers are purple to dark blue in
color and it grows in slightly more moist areas.

☑ **CALIFORNIA BUTTERCUP** . . . . **YELLOW**
   Ranunculus californicus   February-May
FOOTHILL WOODLAND
A 1 to 2 foot perennial herb growing on moist grassy slopes in the
springtime. The numerous flower petals have a waxy sheen. Its latin
name means "little frog" and is probably due to the fact it grows where
frogs are found.

☑ **WESTERN VIRGIN'S BOWER** . . . . **WHITE**
   Clematis ligusticifolia   March-August
FOOTHILL WOODLAND
AND RIPARIAN
A perennial woody vine found climbing into tops of trees and shrubs.
The flowers have no petals but their large white sepals give them a
showy appearance. The spring flowers give rise to long feathery-tailed
seeds which cling together in large fluff-balls that persist through the
summer. An infusion of this plant was used by the Indians for sore
throats and by early settlers to treat sores on their animals.
   78 profuse

☐ **PIPE-STEM** . . . . **GREENISH-WHITE**
   Clematis lasiantha   March-June
CHAPARRAL
Similar to the receding plant except for its small flower and the fact it
grows in moist areas.

☐ **SIERRA MEADOW RUE** . . . . **GREEN to WHITE**
   Thalictrum polycarpum   March-June
FOOTHILL WOODLAND
AND RIPARIAN
A tall delicately leafed herb; often mistaken for Maidenhair Fern. Its
tiny flowers occur in terminal clusters, or *panicles.* An individual flower
is greenish-white, of one sex, without petals and very tiny. It grows in
moist shady places.

MALLOW FAMILY

☐ **FALSE MALLOW** . . . . **LIGHT PINK**
   Malacothamnus Abbottii   June-October
FOOTHILL WOODLAND
A perennial 3 to 7 feet tall with softly-woolly round to oval leaves up
to 2 inches long. Foliage color is pale green. The flowers are ¾ to 1 inch
across, rose-pink, and have the characteristic appearance of all mallows.
If you raise Rose of Sharon, or Hibiscus, the flower resembles this but
is not as large.

GERANIUM FAMILY

☐ **RED-STEMMED FILAREE** or **CRANESBILL**   **ROSE-LAVENDER**
Erodium cicutarium   May-July
FOOTHILL WOODLAND
An annual with pinnately dissected leaves occuring in a circular whorl close to the ground. The hairy leaves are ½ to 5 inches long. Its small flowers are in clusters of 3 to 5 with the petals spotted at their bases. The style is elongated into a ¾ to 1½ inch beak-like shape which resembles a crane's bill.

☐ **PINK FLAX** . . . .**PALE PINK to WHITE**
Linum micranthum   May-July
FOOTHILL WOODLAND
A mini-flowered, mini-leaved herb up to 1 foot tall; most of the height consisting of the flower cluster. The flowers are in a loose spike, which branches from the base, with long-stemmed flowers.

SPURGE FAMILY

☐ **TURKEY MULLEIN** . . . . **GREENISH-WHITE**
Eremocarpus setigerus   May-October
CHAPARRAL AND
FOOTHILL WOODLAND
A common herb growing in rounded clumps 1-3 feet wide and 1-2 inches high. The same-colored flowers and foliage are covered by whitish hairs. There are no petals; only petal-like bracts. Male flowers are cup-like and the female flowers grow in the axils of the flower bracts. Its milky sap, or the whole plant, was used by Indians to stupify fish so they could be caught by hand.

☐ **SPURGE** . . . . **GREENISH-WHITE**
Euphorbia ocellata   May-October
FOOTHILL WOODLAND
Similar to the preceding plant except its foliage is not hairy and, in the flowers cluster, the female flower is surrounded by single stamened male flowers; seeming to grow out of them.

LOASA FAMILY

☐ **MENTZELIA** . . . . **YELLOW**
Mentzelia gracilenta   March-May
XERIC
A 1 to 1½ foot high annual with satiny-yellow 5 petaled flowers. The finely dissected leaves are prickly-hairy and occur in a whorl at its base but alternate further up the stem. It is found in rocky, sunny places.

VIOLET FAMILY

☐ **JOHNNY JUMP-UP** or **YELLOW PANSY** . . . . **YELLOW**
Viola pedunculata   February-April
FOOTHILL WOODLAND
A graceful yellow violet with purple markings on the inner petals and brown markings on the underside of the outer petals. This perennial is found on grassy slopes.

POPPY FAMILY

☐ **CREAM CUPS** . . . . **CREAMY-WHITE**
Platystemon californicus   March-May
FOOTHILL WOODLAND
Single cream-colored flowers occur on stems up to 8 inches high in
early spring. It is a low herb with opposite entire leaves and occurs in
grassy areas.

☑ **TREE POPPY** . . . . **YELLOW**
Dendromecon rigida   April-September
CHAPARRAL
A large evergreen shrub up to 8 feet tall with sparse long willow-like
leaves. Its bright yellow 1 inch flowers occur from late spring to early
fall.

☑ **CALIFORNIA POPPY** . . . . **DARK GOLDEN-YELLOW**
Eschscholtzia californica   February-June
CHAPARRAL AND
FOOTHILL WOODLAND
This state-flower of California is a low growing annual with finely
dissected leaves. It may bloom twice, with the second bloom a much
lighter yellow than the first.

☑ **WIND POPPY** . . . . **ORANGE-RED**
Stylomecon heterophylla   April-May
FOOTHILL WOODLAND
An annual herb larger than the California Poppy, it grows up to 2 feet
tall. The spring flowers have 4 orange-red petals with a purple spot at
the base of each, are less than 1 inch across, and grow in grassy areas.
Beautiful, only a few

FUMITORY FAMILY

☐ **GOLDEN EAR DROPS** . . . . **YELLOW**
Dicentra chrysantha   April-June
CHAPARRAL AND
FOOTHILL WOODLAND
A bright-yellow flowering herb with highly dissected leaves. The slightly
heart-shaped flowers are borne in spikes with individual flowers
nodding or drooping their heads. They are often found on burned-over
areas.

MUSTARD FAMILY

☐ **THELYPODIUM** . . . . **PALE YELLOW**
Thelypodium lasiophyllum   March-June
CHAPARRAL AND
FOOTHILL WOODLAND
Though up to 4 feet tall, it is an inconspicuous plant with yellowish
flower clusters at its top. The fruit is an elongated silique resembling a
miniature pea pod.

☐ **JEWEL FLOWER** . . . . **PURPLE-BROWN**
Streptanthus glandulosus   April-May
CHAPARRAL AND
FOOTHILL WOODLAND
A tall spindly plant with vase-shaped flowers on one side of several loose spikes. Often seen along the trails.

☐ **COMMON PEPPER GRASS** . . . . **WHITE**
Lepidium nitidum   February-May
CHAPARRAL
A small herb, about 1 foot tall, with spikes of miniature flowers. Fruits are round and resemble pepper kernels.

☐ **FIELD MUSTARD** . . . . **YELLOW**
Brassica campestris   January-May
FOOTHILL WOODLAND
A plant up to 6 feet tall with large pinnately compound leaves. The yellow flowers are those you often see in vineyards and orchards on your way to the Pinnacles.

☐ **WINTER CRESS** . . . . **YELLOW**
Barbarea vulgaris   April-May
RIPARIAN
A 16 inch tall flowered mustard with large pinnately compound leaves. Flowers occur in loose terminal spikes.

☐ **WATER CRESS** . . . . **WHITE**
Nasturtium officinale   March-November
RIPARIAN
This plant grows in the water, has small flowers, and pinnately lobed leaves with 3 to 9 rounded lobes. It came to this country from Europe and makes a fine salad.

☐ **TOOTHWORT** . . . . **WHITE to PALE ROSE**
Dentaria californica   February-May
FOOTHILL WOODLAND
One of the first spring flowers; grows in moist shady spots. Flowers are about ½ inch across, leaves are elongate, and the bottom leaves have a tooth-like projection at their base, hence the name.

☐ **FRINGEPOD** . . . . **WHITE to PALE ROSE**
Thysanocarpus curvipes   March-May
CHAPARRAL AND
FOOTHILL WOODLAND
Just over 12 inches, its very long flowering spikes bear tiny flowers. The basal leaves form a circular whorl and the rounded seed pods have fine indentations which give them a fringed appearance.

☐ **BREWER'S ROCK CRESS** . . . . **PINK to PURPLE**
Arabis Breweri   March-July
                                  XERIC
A 2 to 6 inch plant growing in small clumps or dense tufts with small
flowers, very elongate fruit, and hairy foliage.

☑ **WESTERN WALLFLOWER** . . . . **DARK YELLOW to ORANGE**
Erysimum capitatum   March-July
                          XERIC, CHAPARRAL,
                          FOOTHILL WOODLAND
A tall plant with flowers borne in long, cylindrical, round-topped
clusters on long stems. The ¾ inch flowers are usually orange and the
leaves grow in a rosette at the base but are opposite farther up the stem.

PINK FAMILY

☐ **MOUSE-EARED CHICKWEED** . . . . **WHITE**
Cerastium viscosum   February-May
                          CHAPARRAL AND
                          FOOTHILL WOODLAND
A 3 to 10 inch small-leaved herbaceous plant with tiny flowers. Often
found along the road.

☐ **SANDWORT** . . . . **WHITE**
Arenaria Douglasii   April-June
                          CHAPARRAL AND
                          FOOTHILL WOODLAND
A 2 to 8 inch high plant with its leaves and stems thread-like in
appearance. It has numerous very small flowers and gets its name from
the fact it grows in very poor sandy soils.

☐ **WINDMILL PINK** . . . . **WHITE**
Silene gallica   February-June
                          CHAPARRAL AND
                          FOOTHILL WOODLAND
A typical wild pink with 1 to 1½ inch flowers. The flower petals are
twisted nearly ¼ turn; thus resembling the blades of a windmill. It
grows to 15 inches high.

PORTULACA (MOSS-ROSE) FAMILY

☑ **BITTERROOT** . . . . **PINK to WHITE**
Lewisia rediviva   March-June
                          FOOTHILL WOODLAND
                                  XERIC
The 3 inch long, cylindrical, succulent leaves of this plant grow in a
whorl from a shallow thick tap-root. The showy flowers have 13 to 15
petals, grow from a leafless stem, measure up to 2 inches across, and
vary in color.

Beautiful, only a few

27

☐ **RED MAIDS** . . . . **ROSE-RED**
Calandrinia ciliata   February-May
CHAPARRAL AND
FOOTHILL WOODLAND
An early blooming spring flower in grassy spots. Its bright petals open in the sun and close in the shade.

☐ **MINER'S LETTUCE** . . . . **WHITE**
Montia perfoliata   February-May
RIPARIAN AND
FOOTHILL WOODLAND
A somewhat succulent plant easily recognizable by its round perfoliate leaf which completely encircles the stem top. Small flowers grow out of the center of the upper leaf. It occurs in moist shaded places.

BUCKWHEAT FAMILY

☐ **TURKISH RUGGING** . . . . **PINK and WHITE**
Chorizanthe membranacea   April-July
CHAPARRAL AND
FOOTHILL WOODLAND
A 1 to 1½ ft. flowering annual which grows in somewhat grassy areas. Flowers have no petals but colored sepals arranged in pinkish balls or umbels, growing from axils of the stem leaves.

☐ **TURKS RUG** . . . . **DEEP ROSE to LAVENDER**
Chorizanthe Douglasii   April-July
CHAPARRAL AND
FOOTHILL WOODLAND
A much smaller plant than the preceding with similar, but much darker colored, flowers borne only in terminal clusters. Ball-like heads are quite prickly, due to the sharp pointed sepals comprising the colored part of the flowers.

☐ **ERIOGONUM** . . . . **YELLOWISH**
Eriogonum vimineum   June-September
XERIC
A 3 to 18 inch high plant with a much branched flower stem and leaves in a whorl at the base of the plant. Small inconspicuous flowers occur 1 to 5 at a time at the nodes of leafless stems.

☐ **ERIOGONUM** . . . . **RED-BROWN**
Eriogonum Baileyi   May-September
RIPARIAN
Small flowers on leafless, much-branched stems similar to the preceding except the basal leaves are woolly-white and it grows in moist sandy-gravelly places.

☐ **ERIOGONUM** . . . . **ROSE-WHITE**
Eriogonum Nortonii   May-June
CHAPARRAL AND
FOOTHILL WOODLAND
Resembles the preceding two plants except it has smaller reddish stems,
rose-white flowers, and longer stemmed leaves.

☐ **WHITE-LEAFED ERIOGONUM** . . . . **YELLOW**
Eriogonum saxatile   May-July
XERIC
A perennial with a thick woody tap-root and whorls of oval
woolly-white leaves around the base of the woody stem. Balls of flowers
are borne at the nodes of erect branching stems about a foot above the
ground.

☐ **ERIOGONUM** . . . . **WHITISH**
Eriogonum elongatum   August-November
XERIC
A 1 to 4 ft. high shrub with a branching base of leafy stems which give
rise to elongated flowering stems. Balls of tiny flowers occur along
widely separated nodes on the upper stems. Leaves and branches are
woolly-white.

☐ **ERIOGONUM** . . . . **WHITISH**
Eriogonum latifolium   June-November
XERIC
A 1 to 3 ft. shrub similar to the preceding except the stems are smooth
and the oblong leaves are whorled around the base of the plant rather
than on lower branches.

☐ **CALIFORNIA BUCKWHEAT** . . . . **WHITE to PINK**
Eriogonum fasciculatum   May-October
FOOTHILL WOODLAND
A spreading woody shrub with somewhat flattened top, needle-like
leaves, and flowers in compound ball-like clusters. Flowers are mostly
white at first, but turn russet when mature. It is a good honey producer
and the ants seem to prize its seeds and flower-sepals.

☐ **WILLOW DOCK** . . . . **WHITISH**
Rumex salicifolius   May-September
RIPARIAN
This low annual herb grows in moist sandy streambeds. The tall floral
spike bears tiny inconspicuous flowers which eventually produce a
characteristic rust-red, dock-like fruiting spike with triangular winged
seeds. The name is from its thin elongated willow-like leaves.

29

☐ **CURLY DOCK** . . . . **WHITISH**
Rumex crispus   All Year
RIPARIAN
An exotic 1 to 4 ft. high plant with long wavy green leaves. The tall
flowering spike barely shows its flowers but as seeds mature and enlarge
it takes on a rusty-red color. You will find it in streambeds. In some
places it is cultivated as a source of tannic acid.

PRIMROSE FAMILY

☑ **SHOOTING STAR** . . . . **ROSE, PURPLE, or WHITE**
Dodecatheon Hendersonii   February-May
FOOTHILL WOODLAND
One of the more striking early spring flowers with its backward reflexed
petals, and stamens united in a point at the forward end giving an
appearance of motion. Blackish stamens have a white or yellow ring
between them and the 5 petals. Flowers are borne on long, thick,
hollow, red-colored stems, and leaves also possess a fairly long stem.
The root crown produces tiny rice-sized bulblets which give rise to new
plants.

☐ **SHOOTING STAR** . . . . **ROSE, PURPLE, or WHITE**
Dodecatheon Clevelandii   January-April
XERIC AND
CHAPARRAL
Probably the earliest spring flower; differing from the above in having
no rice-like bublets, a non-red stem, and a much smaller size with
stemless appearing leaves.

☐ **SCARLET PIMPERNELL** . . . . **ORANGE-RED**
Anagallis arvensis . . . . March-July
FOOTHILL WOODLAND
A low prostrate plant with small, opposite, oval leaves and flowers
found low in the grass.

PLANTAIN FAMILY

☐ **PLANTAIN** . . . . **PEARLY-WHITE**
Plantago Hookeriana   March-May
FOOTHILL WOODLAND
A small annual with ribbed, quasi-parallel-veined leaves which are long,
narrow, and covered with fine hair. Tiny flowers in the spikes have 4
petals, sepals, stamens, and pistils.

HEATH FAMILY

☐ **MEXICAN MANZANITA** . . . . **PINK or WHITE**
Arctostaphylos pungens   February-March
CHAPARRAL
This large shrub is one of the main members of the Chaparral
community. Its bark is conspicuous by its coppery-red color and the
fact it peels off in very thin strips or flakes. Leaves are dark-green,

pointed-oval, and smooth. Flowers are small, vase-shaped, and hang downward. The fruit is about ¼ inch in diameter with the color and shape of a small apple; in fact, the Spanish word "manzanita" means little apple.

☑ **BIG-BERRIED MANZANITA** . . . . **PINK and WHITE**
Arctostaphylos glauca December-March
CHAPARRAL
Often larger than the preceding shrub to the point of being almost tree size, its bark and flowers are very much like those of the preceding plant. The main differences are the almost circular gray-green leaves and the big (¾ inch) berries. Berries of both shrubs have often been used as food. They taste like a very bland, mealy apple.

GENTIAN FAMILY
☐ **TALL CENTAU** . . . . **PINK**
Centaurium exaltatum May-August
CHAPARRAL AND
FOOTHILL WOODLAND
A small plant with clusters of small pink flowers which have 5 oval petals united into a tube at their base. Its leaves are also oval and medium green.

OLIVE FAMILY
☐ **FLOWERING ASH** . . . . **WHITE**
Fraxinus dipetala April-May
CHAPARRAL
A small tree growing in and near washes on mountain slopes. Unlike other ash trees, their flowers are showy with an upper and lower petal. Fruits are double, each having wings like half a maple seed. Like most ashes, the leaves are pinnately compound with 3 to 9 leaflets.

☐ **DESERT OLIVE** . . . . **GREENISH**
Forestiera neomexicana March-April
CHAPARRAL
This is a 5 to 10 ft. shrub having simple oval leaves with toothed edges and opposite to each other. The tiny flowers have no petals, very small sepals, and give rise to a blue-black, pitted, olive-like fruit about 1/3 inch long. These occur in clusters along somewhat spiny branches.

MILKWEED FAMILY
☐ **MEXICAN MILKWEED** . . . . **WHITE**
Asclepias fascicularis June-September
RIPARIAN
Our species grows in or near dry streambeds, has long narrow leaves in whorls of 4, clusters of typical milkweed flowers, milky sap, and long narrow seed-pods which emit fluffy seeds in the fall. Indians used the juice to make a chewing gum and the fibers for string and cord but probably didn't use this species much because of its small size.

31

MORNING GLORY FAMILY

☐ **PURPLE-RIBBED MORNING GLORY** . . . . **WHITE**
Convolvulus subacaulis   April-June
CHAPARRAL
A trailing vine, or short prostrate plant, with heart-shaped leaves and
morning glory type flowers. Flowers are white on the inside with purple
folds, or ribs, on the outside.

☐ **COMMON MORNING GLORY** . . . . **WHITE or PINK**
Convolvulus occidentalis   May-September
RIPARIAN
A tall climbing vine with arrow-shaped leaves that are somewhat hairy.
The flowers age to a purple color.

DODDER FAMILY

☑ **DODDER** . . . . **ORANGE-YELLOW**
Cuscuta brachycalyx   June-September
FOOTHILL WOODLAND
Dodder is a nearly leafless parasite with no chlorophyll and totally
dependent on its host plant, which is usually the California Buckwheat
here. It bears flowers that produce seeds which sprout in the earth and
allow the plant to grow until it can become attached to its host plant. It
then breaks contact with the earth and lives completely off its host
forming a tangled mass of orangish threads.

PHLOX FAMILY

☐ **MICROSTERIS** . . . . **WHITE to LAVENDER**
Microsteris gracilis   March-August
FOOTHILL WOODLAND
A small delicate annual less than 1 ft. tall with oblong-elliptical leaves
about 1/3 inch long and tiny 5-petaled funnel-shaped flowers which are
yellow inside.

☐ **GLOBE GILIA** . . . . **BLUE to VIOLET**
Gilia capitata   May-July
FOOTHILL WOODLAND
A beautiful blue wildflower with round globes of flowers on a long
stem. Individual flowers have 5 petals united at the base into a tube. The
1 to 4 inch leaves are once or twice pinnate. You will find them in
grassy meadows.

☐ **DWARF GILIA or YELLOW GILIA** . . . . **BLUE to PINK**
Gilia achillaefolia   May-June
CHAPARRAL AND
FOOTHILL WOODLAND
A small annual 6 to 12 inches tall with individual flowers like the
preceding ones but only 2 to 7 per cluster. Petals vary in color and are
yellow on the lower inside of the tube. Leaves are in a basal whorl and
finely dissected like yarrow leaves.

☐ **GILIA** . . . . **BLUE**
Eriastrum densifolium   May-July
CHAPARRAL

Tall, woody-stemmed, much-branched perennials bearing round heads of 25 or more flowers similar in form to true gilias except the sepals have pointed tips making flowers prickly to the touch. Inside, the corolla tube is yellow. The needle-like leaves have a terminal and 4 lateral spines. The entire plant is covered with fuzzy white hair.

☐ **GILIA** . . . . **BLUE**
Eriastrum virgatum   May-July
CHAPARRAL AND
FOOTHILL WOODLAND

Similar to the preceding plant but an annual that is less branching and is smaller in size.

☐ **PRICKLY GILIA** . . . . **BLUE**
Navarretia mitracarpa   April-June
CHAPARRAL

A low branching annual with clusters of gilia-like flowers. It has spiny bracts and very spiny, broad, thistle-like leaves. A cottony fuzz on stems and in flower heads is a characteristic of this species.

☐ **STICKY PRICKLY GILIA** . . . . **BLUE**
Navarretia atractyloides   May-July
CHAPARRAL AND
FOOTHILL WOODLAND

Much like the preceding plant except the foliage is covered with sticky glandular hairs making the plant sticky, as well as prickly, to the touch.

☐ **PIGMY LINANTHUS** . . . . **WHITE**
Linanthus pygmaeus   April-June
CHAPARRAL AND
FOOTHILL WOODLAND

A tiny, delicate, much-branched plant with minute flowers and leaves. Its flowers have 5 petals united into a corolla tube; leaves are composed of 3 needle-like lobes.

☐ **EVENING SNOW** . . . . **WHITE**
Linanthus dichotomus   April-June
CHAPARRAL AND
FOOTHILL WOODLAND

A flower easily mistaken for white phlox. It grows to 9 inches on thin stems with long, needle-like leaves and single flowers about 1 inch wide with 5 petals united at the bottom into a corolla tube.

☐ **LINANTHUS** . . . .**BLUE**
Linanthus ciliatus April-July
CHAPARRAL AND
FOOTHILL WOODLAND
This species has many-flowered heads with numerous bracts. Small, individual flowers have 5 petals and a corolla tube 3 times as long as the petals. The downy linear leaves are arranged in whorls around the stem.

☐ **LINANTHUS** . . . .**BLUE**
Linanthus androsaceus April-June
CHAPARRAL AND
FOOTHILL WOODLAND
A delicately formed annual with larger more showy flowers than the preceding plant, in many-flowered heads of 8 to 15 each. The ½ inch flowers stand away from the heads on small stems and resemble small phlox with their linear leaves arranged in whorls around the stem.

WATERLEAF FAMILY

☐ **FIESTA FLOWER** . . . . **PURPLE**
Pholistoma auritum March-May
CHAPARRAL AND
FOOTHILL WOODLAND
This sprawling annual has 1-inch flowers and highly dissected leaves that are somewhat fern-like in appearance. Its stem is 4-angled and diamond-shaped in cross-section. The entire plant has weak recurved spines which tend to cause it to cling to your clothes. You will find it in shady spots.

☐ **WHITE NEMOPHILA** . . . .**WHITE with PURPLE SPOTS**
Pholistoma membranaceum March-May
CHAPARRAL AND
FOOTHILL WOODLAND
A prostrate flower with smooth non-hairy foliage. Flowers are similar to Baby Blue-Eyes but differ in color.

☐ **ELLISIA** . . . . **WHITE to YELLOW**
Eucrypta chrysanthemifolia March-June
RIPARIAN AND FOOTHILL WOODLAND
A 12-inch plant with delicately dissected leaves having an unpleasant odor, an adaptation which keeps them from being eaten. Loose bunches of ¼ inch flowers resemble those of White Nemophila.

☑ **BABY BLUE-EYES** . . . .**BLUE with WHITE CENTER**
Nemophila Menziesii February-June
FOOTHILL WOODLAND
A low prostrate annual growing in grassy areas in late spring and early summer. Delicate 5-petaled flowers are about 1½ inches across with highly dissected compound leaves which are usually well concealed in the grass making the flowers more prominent than usual.

34

☐ **WILD HELIOTROPE** . . . . .BLUE
Phacelia distans   March-June
FOOTHILL WOODLAND
A 1½ ft. annual with broadly bell-shaped flowers occuring in clusters.
Individual flowers have a family resemblance to Baby Blue-Eyes but
have fuzzy or hairy foliage.

☐ **STINGING PHACELIA** . . . . WHITE
Phacelia Rattanii   May-July
CHAPARRAL
Flowers similar to Wild Heliotrope, except for color, growing in slender
½-2 inch spikes. Foliage is bristly and stinging to the touch.

☐ **ROCK PHACELIA** . . . . LAVENDER
Phacelia californica   April-July
CHAPARRAL AND
FOOTHILL WOODLAND
An annual with flowers in long many-flowered heads with new buds
near the upper end curling under like a violin handle. Flowers are all on
the upper side of the stem.

☐ **PHACELIA** . . . . WHITE, PINK or LAVENDER
Phacelia brachyloba   May-June
CHAPARRAL
An annual with short-hairy glandular foliage, linear to oblong leaves,
and bell-shaped flowers with yellow throats. Flowers occur in dense
spikes.

☐ **WHISPERING BELLS** . . . . CREAM to YELLOW
Emmenanthe penduliflora   April-July
CHAPARRAL AND
FOOTHILL WOODLAND
A ½-2 ft. annual with fern-shaped, or pinnatified, leaves. Its delicate
drooping bell-shaped flowers occur in loose bunches.

☑ **YERBA SANTA** . . . . .WHITE to BLUE
Eriodictyon californicum   May-July
CHAPARRAL
A shrub up to 5 feet high with elongate leaves having toothed edges and
clusters of flowers with their 5 petals united into a long, funnel-shaped,
corolla tube. It has been highly valued by many for its medicinal
properties. Colds and other respiratory ailments were treated with a
brew of its leaves.

☑ **WOOLLY YERBA SANTA** . . . . WHITISH
Eriodictyon tomentosum   June-July
CHAPARRAL AND
FOOTHILL WOODLAND
Similar to above but covered with dense woolly hair.

35

☐ **WOOLLY YERBA SANTA** . . . . **LAVENDER**
Eriodictyon crassifolium   April-June
CHAPARRAL
A 3-10 ft. shrub much like the preceding except its flowers are different
colored and larger; measuring ½ inch in length.

FORGET-ME-NOT FAMILY

☐ **WHITE FORGET-ME-NOT** . . . . **WHITE**
Cryptantha muricata   April-June
CHAPARRAL AND FOOTHILL WOODLAND
A ½-1 ft. erect-branching annual with dense flower spikes. Each flower
measures about 1/3 inch across. Linear leaves are stiffly hairy, and fruit
consists of 4 nut-like seeds, a characteristic of this family.

☐ **POPCORN FLOWER** . . . . **WHITE**
Plagiobothrys nothofulvus   March-May
CHAPARRAL AND
FOOTHILL WOODLAND
Very much like the preceding except its roots, stems, and leaves contain
a purple dye which gives it a generally purplish color. It is very common
in the spring.

☐ **POPCORN FLOWER** . . . . **WHITE**
Plagiobothrys canescens   March-May
FOOTHILL WOODLAND
A prostrate herb with flowers like those of the preceding 2 plants but in
loose spikes. Its hairy foliage is purplish but not as much so as *P.
nothofulvus.*

☐ **POPCORN FLOWER** . . . . **WHITE**
Plagiobothrys californicus   March-May
FOOTHILL WOODLAND
A light green plant with no dye in its foliage. The spreading prostrate
stems have tiny flowers at their ends.

☑ **FIDDLENECK** . . . . **ORANGE-YELLOW**
Amsinckia Douglasiana   March-May
FOOTHILL WOODLAND
An erect 12-15 inch annual with flower spikes which curl under at the
tip like a fiddle-neck. Linear leaves are covered with white bristles and
it is the only member of this family here, bearing gray instead of black
seeds.

☐ **FIDDLENECK** . . . . **ORANGE-YELLOW**
Amsinckia intermedia   March-June
FOOTHILL WOODLAND
The only noticeable difference between this and the previous plant is
the black seed it bears.

NIGHTSHADE FAMILY

☐ **CHAPARRAL NIGHTSHADE** . . . . **PURPLE-BLUE**
Solanum umbelliferum   January-June
CHAPARRAL AND
FOOTHILL WOODLAND
This perennial shrub has star-shaped flowers united into a tube at the back. Bright yellow anthers clustered together at the center are strikingly contrasted with purple flowers. Gray hairy foliage provides a good backdrop for the flowers. You will find it in gullies.

☐ **SACRED DATURA** . . . . **WHITE to PALE LAVENDER**
Datura meteloides   April-October
FOOTHILL WOODLAND
Large heart-shaped leaves of this 2-3 ft. plant with large trumpet-shaped flowers make it easy to recognize. The seeds in its round spiny green fruit contain hallucination producing alkaloid which is quite poisonous and usually deadly. American Indians used this plant in religious rites, with frequently fatal results.

☐ **INDIAN TOBACCO** . . . . **WHITE**
Nicotiana Bigelovii   May-October
FOOTHILL WOODLAND
A large 1-5 ft. plant with strong-scented leaves and large trumpet-shaped flowers about 2 inches long. Indians used the leaves for smoking and medicine.

☐ **COYOTE TOBACCO** . . . . **WHITE**
Nicotiana attenuata   May-October
FOOTHILL WOODLAND
Similar to the preceding plant except for wavy-edged leaves and smaller flowers. It had the same uses.

SNAPDRAGON FAMILY

☐ **SCARLET MONKEY FLOWER** . . . . **RED**
Mimulus cardinalis   April-October
RIPARIAN
An attractive 2-lipped flower with the frontal appearance of a monkey face. Foliage is quite hairy.

☐ **YELLOW MONKEY FLOWER** . . . . **YELLOW**
Mimulus floribundus   April-August
RIPARIAN
The small 1/3 inch flowers of this plant have 2 black spots on the upper center petal. Foliage is covered with soft small hairs and it has a musky odor.

☐ **COMMON YELLOW MONKEY FLOWER** . . . . .**YELLOW with**
PURPLE SPOTS
Mimulus guttatus March-August
RIPARIAN
These flowers are larger than the preceding and have purple spots in
their throats. Indians used the green tender leaves as a salad and roots
to prepare an astringent.

☐ **DESERT MONKEY FLOWER** . . . . **ROSE-PURPLE**
Mimulus Fremontii April-June
CHAPARRAL AND
FOOTHILL WOODLAND
A 6 inch annual with ½-3/4 inch flowers. Stems are much shorter than
flowers at first, but later become much branched and achieve their full
height.

☐ **CHAPARRAL MONKEY FLOWER** . . . . **ROSE-PURPLE**
Mimulus Rattanii May-July
CHAPARRAL
The difference between this plant and the preceding one is it has a
longer seed capsule, a shorter calyx tube, and grows mostly on recently
burned areas.

☐ **STICKY MONKEY FLOWER** . . . . **ORANGE-YELLOW**
Mimulus auranticus March-August
CHAPARRAL
A low woody shrub with small linear leaves that are sticky to the touch.
The flower may vary from a dark orange to a buff color and is seen
mostly in rocky areas.

☐ **SCARLET BUGLER** . . . . **BRIGHT SCARLET**
Penstemon centranthifolius April-July
FOOTHILL WOODLAND
A 1-3 ft. annual with several bare stems having loose spikes of tubular
flowers barely open at the end. Not obviously 2-lipped.

☐ **VIOLET BEARD-TONGUE** . . . . **VIOLET to BLUE**
Penstemon heterophyllus April-July
CHAPARRAL AND
FOOTHILL WOODLAND
A woody based annual growing in clumps with stems to 2 ft.
Violet-tubed flowers have bluish outer petals. Leaves are finely hairy
and linear in shape.

☐ **GAPING PENSTEMON** . . . . **PINK-STRIPED WHITE**
Penstemon breviflorus May-July
CHAPARRAL
A spindly perennial woody shrub up to 9 ft. tall. Gaping, slightly
tubular flowers are marked along outer edges of their petals. Though
tall, the plant is inconspicuous.

☐ **CALIFORNIA BEE PLANT** . . . . **REDDISH-BROWN**
Scrophularia californica   February-July
FOOTHILL WOODLAND
A favorite of bees, this 3-6 ft. plant is often cultivated by bee keepers.
Basal leaves are about 4 inches long but shorten as they go up the stem.
Small inconspicous flowers are clustered at the plant tips.

☑ **CHINESE HOUSES** . . . . **ROSE-PURPLE, PALE
LILAC or WHITE**
Collinsia concolor   April-June
FOOTHILL WOODLAND
An annual with 2-lipped flowers; 2 upper and 3 lower lobes. The upper
lobes are light, the lower darker colored. Flowers occur in a circular
whorl around the stem, each tier smaller than the one below it, thus
giving the appearance of a pagoda, or Chinese house.

☐ **SIERRA SNAPDRAGON** . . . . **ROSE-RED**
Antirrhinum multiflorum   May-July
CHAPARRAL AND
FOOTHILL WOODLAND
Flowers resemble those of domestic snapdragons. Cream-colored palates
close the flower throats. The flowers occur in spikes.

☐ **VIOLET SNAPDRAGON** . . . . **LAVENDER to VIOLET**
Antirrhinum vexillo   May-July
CHAPARRAL
The roughly hairy foliage of this plant, closed throats, and spurs at the
base of the flower tube, plus the fact it grows almost exclusively on
burned areas, identifies this plant.

☐ **BLUE SNAPDRAGON** . . . . **BLUE OUTSIDE:
DEEP VIOLET INSIDE**
Antirrhinum Kelloggii   March-May
CHAPARRAL
Another snapdragon of burned areas but smooth foliaged with vine-like
twining upper stems. The flower palate is fuzzy.

☐ **INDIAN-WARRIOR** . . . . **DEEP RED**
Pedicularis densiflora   January-June
CHAPARRAL
One of the earliest spring flowers; often mistaken for Indian Paintbrush.
Fern-like leaves are bronze colored when they first emerge turning
green later. The plant is a partial parasite of Chamise-Greasewood.

☐ **OWL CLOVER** . . . . **PINK to PURPLE**
Orthocarpus purpurascens   March-May
FOOTHILL WOODLAND
Not a true clover, this foot high plant has short, feathery, needle-like
leaves extending up into the flower head in the form of pink bracts near
the top. The narrow flowers vary in color.

☑ **INDIAN PAINTBRUSH** . . . **YELLOW FLOWER in RED CUP**
Castilleja affinis   March-May
CHAPARRAL AND
FOOTHILL WOODLAND
A wildflower familiar to many which looks red but on close inspection reveals a yellow flower deeply seated in red bracts. It too is partially parasitic on woody plant roots.

☑ **WOOLLY INDIAN PAINTBRUSH** . . . . **RED TIP with**
YELLOW MIDDLE
Castilleja foliolosa   March-May
CHAPARRAL
Similar to the above but with a more open flower cluster and white-woolly foliage.

BROOMRAPE FAMILY

☐ **BROOMRAPE** . . . . **BROWNISH**
Orobanche bulbosa   April-July
CHAPARRAL
An odd stout dark-colored plant 3-4 ft. high which lacks chlorophyll and is fully parasitic on roots of many shrubs. Flowers range from yellow to brownish and occur in spikes.

MINT FAMILY

☐ **CAMPHOR-WEED or VINEGAR-WEED** . . . .**BLUE**
Trichostema lanceolatum   August-October
FOOTHILL WOODLAND
A fragrant leafy herb up to 16 inches tall with 2-lipped flowers in a spike along the stem. Tubular flowers are strongly recurved at the end, like a hook, with long curving stamens issuing from the center of the flower throat. It is an important bee plant.

☐ **WOOLLY BLUE-CURLS** . . . . **BLUE**
Trichostema lanatum   May-August
CHAPARRAL
A 2-4 ft. woody shrub with narrow aromatic 2 inch leaves. Flower buds appear to be covered with pink and blue velvet flocking and the 2-lipped flowers have extremely long curving stamens issuing from their throat. This plant has been used as an astringent and a remedy for ulcerated sores.

☐ **BLUE SKULLCAP** . . . . **BLUE**
Scutellaria tuberosa   March-July
FOOTHILL WOODLAND
A 3/4 inch long 2-lipped flower with the upper lip shaped like a hood or cap. This 6 inch plant grows in shaded areas and has roots which form small fleshy underground tubers.

☐ **COMMON HOREHOUND** . . . . **WHITE**
Marrubium vulgare   April-September
ALL COMMUNITIES
An erect plant up to 2 ft. high; all parts are covered with white-woolly fuzz. Roundish leaves are edged with blunt teeth and have a pebble-grained surface. Tiny white flowers occur in interrupted spikes with button-like heads separated by bare stem, and are typically 2-lipped. Sepals form a tube with 10 prickly tips. The tops are used as a cold remedy and it flavors horehound candy.

☑ **HEDGENETTLE** . . . . **WHITE to PURPLE**
Stachys bullata   April-September
RIPARIAN
A 5-10 ft. herb with white-woolly foliage and oval leaves. The 2-lipped flowers grow in 3-9 inch spikes along streams.

☑ **CHIA** . . . . **DARK BLUE**
Salvia Columbariae   March-June
CHAPARRAL AND
FOOTHILL WOODLAND
An errect herb up to 18 inches high with dark green, pinnately dissected leaves. This early spring wildflower has bright colored flowers on an interrupted spike having 1-4 button-like heads separated by bare sections of stem. Bases of the flower spikes are maroon in color. Mature flowers produce large gray seeds which are highly nutritious and valued as a food source by the Indians. They are ground and mixed with acorn meal or drunk as a gruel. It has been said a tablespoon of seeds was sufficient to sustain an Indian on a forced march an entire day.

☐ **BLACK SAGE** . . . . **WHITISH**
Salvia mellifera   April-July
CHAPARRAL
A woody shrub with typical mint-like flowers arranged in interrupted spikes of button-like balls separated by intervals of bare stem. The fragrant gray-green foliage is often used as a spice in cooking. It is an important bee plant.

☐ **PITCHER SAGE** . . . . **WHITE**
Lepechinia calycina   April-June
CHAPARRAL
An attractive shrub with large pitcher-shaped flowers, sometimes tinged with pink, which hang downward from the stem. The 1 inch flowers are almost regular, though a 2-lipped shape can be discerned. They are short lived and last only a few days. The broad-shaped, aromatic woolly leaves are wavy-edged.

☐ **COYOTE MINT** . . . . **PURPLE**
Monardella villosa June-August
CHAPARRAL AND
FOOTHILL WOODLAND
A fragrant herb with terminal clusters of flowers borne in spherical densely flowered heads. Broad wavy edged leaves are covered with fine hairs. Early Spanish settlers valued these plants as a remedy for many ailments.

STONECROP FAMILY

☐ **PIGMY WEED** . . . . **WHITE**
Tillaea erecta February-May
XERIC
A tiny highly branched succulent with tufts of reddish oval, or teardrop-shaped, leaves and bunches of tiny white flowers.

☐ **MINIATURE SEDUM** . . . . **REDDISH-YELLOW**
Parvisedum pentandrum April-May
XERIC
An erect 2-6 inch succulent with slender stems bearing oblong-shaped reddish-green leaves. Flowers are quite fleshy and crowded together in flat-topped clusters.

☐ **ROCK LETTUCE or LIVE-FOREVER** . . . . . **YELLOW to RED**
Dudleya cymosa May-June
XERIC
A succulent with a crowded basal whorl of gray-green leaves up to 6 inches long. The 5-10 inch flowering stem terminates in clusters of fleshy flowers. Usually on the cliffs.

☐ **STONECROP or ORPIN** . . . . **YELLOW to ORANGE**
sometimes WHITE
Sedum spathulifolium May-July
RIPARIAN
Its roundish blunt-ended leaves occur in rosettes at the end of 4-8 inch stems. Flowers are flat-topped clusters on branched ends of 2-12 inch stems. It is most common on shaded, mossy rocks.

GOOSEBERRY FAMILY

☐ **CALIFORNIA SAXIFRAGE** . . . . **WHITE to ROSE**
Saxifraga californica February-June
CHAPARRAL AND
FOOTHILL WOODLAND
An annual with broad-oval glandular-hairy green leaves in a basal whorl. Its dime-sized star-shaped flowers have 5 petals, 10 stamens, and 2 pistils. They grow in flat-topped clusters on the end of 6-18 inch reddish colored stems.

☐ **WOODLAND STAR** . . . . **WHITE**
  Lithophragma heterophylla   March-June
                    FOOTHILL WOODLAND
An annual with flowers having 5 petals, 10 stamens, and growing in
groups of 3-9 flowers. Petals are often ragged tipped and the base of the
flower tube is flat or cylindrical. Broad-oval basal leaves are shallowly
lobed. Stem leaves are definitely 3 lobed. It grows in shady areas.

☐ **WOODLAND STAR** . . . . **WHITE**
  Lithophragma affinis   March-May
                    CHAPARRAL AND
                    FOOTHILL WOODLAND
Much like the preceding plant except the flowers are always 3-lobed
with a large central lobe and 2 smaller lateral lobes. The base of the
flower is cone-shaped instead of flat. Basal leaves are often bronze
colored and not so hairy.

☐ **CHAPARRAL CURRANT** . . . . **WHITE to PINK**
  Ribes malvaceum   October-March
                    CHAPARRAL
A graceful drooping 4-9 ft. bush with broad thick palmately-lobed
leaves. The gray-green leaves have 3-5 lobes, a fuzzy-white underside,
and are ½-1 inch wide. Flowers occur in spikes of 10-25 at the branch
tips. They have a cylindrical calyx with flower petals inside the calyx
tube. The slightly hairy blue-black berry is sweet and edible. It was a
favorite food of the Indians.

☐ **HILLSIDE GOOSEBERRY** . . . . **CREAM to YELLOW**
  Ribes quercetorum   March-May
                    FOOTHILL WOODLAND
A spiny 2-3 ft. shrub whose flowers occur in groups of 2-3. The 1/3 to
¼ inch wide leaves have 3-5 sharp-pointed palmate lobes. The smooth
black berry was eaten by Indians, mixed with acorn and chia flour.

☐ **SPINY GOOSEBERRY** . . . . . **GREENISH-WHITE to PURPLE**
  Ribes californicum   February-March
                    CHAPARRAL AND
                    FOOTHILL WOODLAND
A spiny 3-10 ft. shrub with 3-5 lobed oval leaves from ½-1½ inches
wide. Flowers occur in groups of 2-3 and their actual color is white; the
apparent color is actually that of the inside surface of the sepals. The
small reddish berry is covered with long slender spines and is edible if
you can get past the spines.

ROSE FAMILY

☐ **STICKY POTENTILLA** . . . . **YELLOW to CREAM**
  Potentilla glandulosa   May-July
                    CHAPARRAL AND
                    FOOTHILL WOODLAND
A perennial woody-based plant with glandular-hairy foliage and reddish
stems. The 5-petaled flowers resemble those of a strawberry with

43

numerous stamens and pistils. The ¼-½ inch wide flowers occur in dense flat-topped clusters. Basal leaves are pinnately compound with 5-9 leaflets.

☑ **CHAMISE or GREASEWOOD** . . . . **WHITE**
Adenostoma fasciculatum May-June
CHAPARRAL
A ubiquitous woody shrub with dark-green short needle-like leaves and bunches of tiny flowers at the stem tips. The bark contains a resinous material which is highly flammable. Indians considered it an excellent remedy for many ailments such as snake-bite, colds, cramps and an infallible cure for tetanus. Foliage was fried in grease to make a healing ointment.

☐ **MOUNTAIN MAHOGANY** . . . . **WHITE to GREENISH**
Cercocarpus betuloides March-May
CHAPARRAL AND
FOOTHILL WOODLAND
A shrub or small tree with toothed oval leaves that are dark green above, woolly-white below, and deeply feather-veined. There are 1-6 tiny flowers, at a time, which produce a characteristic reddish seed with a 3-4 inch feathery tail. Inner bark contains a purple dye much prized by Indians. The entire bark was used to make a cold-cure tea and the entire plant served as a laxative.

☐ **BLACKBERRY** . . . . **WHITE**
Rubus vitifolius March-July
RIPARIAN
Spiny woody canes with characteristic rose-like flowers. It is much like domestic blackberries. Leaves are sometimes mistaken for poison oak. Berries are edible, if you can beat the birds to them.

☐ **WILD ROSE** . . . . **PINK**
Rosa californica May-October
FOOTHILL WOODLAND
A thorny climbing shrub with single flowers about 1 inch across. The fruit, a typical rose hip, is rich in Vitamin C. You will find it near streambeds.

☐ **HOLLY-LEAF CHERRY** . . . . **WHITE**
Prunus ilicifolia April-May
CHAPARRAL
An evergreen shrub with shiny dark-green prickly leaves like those of holly. Creamy white flowers occur in 3-4 inch spikes and the large dark-red fruit is sweet but disappointing, since the seed occupies all but the outer 1/8 inch of the cherry. It is widely eaten by birds, deer, and other wildlife. Indians made an alcoholic drink from it and ground the seed kernel to mix with acorn flour.

☑ **CALIFORNIA HOLLY or TOYON** . . . . **WHITE**
Heteromeles arbutifolia   June-July
CHAPARRAL
An evergreen shrub sometimes confused with holly-leaf cherry. Long leathery leaves and flat-topped flower clusters distinguish it from the other. In fall and winter it bears clusters of bright red ¼ inch berries. Berries are bitter, unless cooked, but were gathered by both Indians and early Spanish settlers as a primary source of food.

PEA FAMILY

☐ **CHAPARRAL PEA** . . . . **BRIGHT PINK**
Pickeringia montana   May-August
CHAPARRAL
An extremely spiny tangled dense 3-8 ft. bush with ¼ inch oval green leaves which are hard and leathery. This variety has a flower color not matching most descriptions. The flower is about 1 inch across and seed pods are rare. The bush occurs in only one or two places here and seems to favor burned-over areas.

☑ **LUPINE** . . . . **PURPLE to ROSE-PINK**
Lupinus subvexus   April-June
FOOTHILL WOODLAND
A ½-2½ ft. annual with uniformly colored flowers. Pinnate compound leaves have 5-9 leaflets with terminal spines, mostly located at the base or middle parts of the stem.

☐ **WHITE VEINED LUPINE** . . . . . . **WHITE with PINK VEINS**
Lupinus densiflorus   April-June
FOOTHILL WOODLAND
A 3/4-2½ ft. annual with pinnately compound leaves of 7-9 leaflets, smooth on the upper surface and softly hairy underneath.

☐ **LUPINE** . . . . **LILAC**
Lupinus concinnus   March-May
CHAPARRAL AND
FOOTHILL WOODLAND
A low 2 to 16 inch annual with dense softly-hairy foliage well distributed over its slender stems. Flowers are edged with red-purple color and its banner has a yellow center. Usually in disturbed or burned areas.

☐ **HOLLOW-LEAF LUPINE** . . . . **BLUE to WHITE**
Lupinus succulentus   February-May
FOOTHILL WOODLAND
A stout succulent lupine with hollow stems and leaves. The 12 to 30 inch plant has variable colored flowers with a yellow centered banner which turns violet on aging. Pinnate leaves have 7 to 10 smooth hairless leaflets.

☐ **WHITE-LEAVED BUSH LUPINE . DARK BLUE to LAVENDER**
Lupinus albifrons   March-June
CHAPARRAL AND
FOOTHILL WOODLAND
A perennial leafy shrub with a silvery-white appearance, caused by fine silky-white hairs which cover it.

☐ **SPOTTED BLUE LUPINE . . . . . .BLUE with a WHITE SPOT**
Lupinus micranthus   March-June
FOOTHILL WOODLAND
A 6 to 18 inch annual with leaves of 5 to 7 leaflets. The name is derived from the white spot on the flower banner.

☐ **BUR CLOVER . . . . YELLOW**
Medicago hispida   March-June
CHAPARRAL AND
FOOTHILL WOODLAND
A spreading clover-like plant with yellow pea-like flowers in groups of 3 to 5 and 3-lobed clover leaves. The conical coiled seed-pod resembles a turban seashell and is covered with barbed stickers. The plant is prized as stock feed.

☐ **BIRDSFOOT TREFOIL . . . . YELLOW**
Lotus salsuginosus   March-June
CHAPARRAL AND
FOOTHILL WOODLAND
A low prostrate-branching plant with pinnate leaves of 5 to 6 leaflets which are slightly succulent and vary from ½ to 1½ inches long. Flowers grow from a common point and number 1 to 5 at a time. Fruit is an elongated pod.

☐ **LOTUS . . . . .PINK to SALMON**
Lotus micranthus   March-May
FOOTHILL WOODLAND
This is similar to the preceding one but has single pinkish flowers and ½ inch leaves with 3 to 5 leaflets. Pods are constricted between seeds, giving them a curved appearance.

☐ **HILL LOTUS . . . . YELLOW**
Lotus humistratus   March-June
FOOTHILL WOODLAND
A low branching plant with pinnate leaves of 3 to 5 leaflets. The single flowers are tinged magenta on aging. Often densely covered with silky hairs.

☐ **HILL LOTUS . . . . YELLOW**
Lotus subpinnatus   March-June
FOOTHILL WOODLAND
Similar to above but larger and less hairy.

46

☐ **CALIFORNIA BROOM or DEERWEED** . . . . .YELLOW
Lotus scoparius   March-August
FOOTHILL WOODLAND
A 1½ to 4 ft. bushy-erect perennial with slender stems rising from a woody base. Mature flowers are tinged with red and grow in whorls around a main stem with no flower stem apparent. The curved seed pod has a hook on the end.

☐ **SAN DIEGO PEA** . . . . .PINK to WHITE
Lathyrus laetiflorus   April-June
CHAPARRAL AND
FOOTHILL WOODLAND
A prostrate vine with pinnate compound leaves of 8 to 12 oblong leaflets and numerous coiling tendrils, growing along streambeds. The large flowers resemble those of domestic sweet peas and occur singly on a short stem. The 2-inch pods have many seeds.

SYCAMORE FAMILY

☐ **WESTERN SYCAMORE** . . . . .INCONSPICUOUS
Platanus racemosa   February-April
RIPARIAN
A large deciduous tree with typical sycamore bark of large white plates which scale and fall off. The very large leaves exceed 6 inches across and have 5 points arranged like the palm of a hand. They are light green above and covered with woolly white fuzz below. In fall the leaves turn golden. The fruit is a round prickly ball about 1½ inches across.

OAK FAMILY

☑ **COAST LIVE OAK** . . . . .CATKINS
Quercus agrifolia   March-April
RIPARIAN
A large evergreen oak with thick shiny dark-green leaves which are prickly edged and cupped downward. Leaves measure 3/4 to 4 inches long by ½ to 3 inches wide. The tree grows to 30 ft. in height and the dark-gray bark is broken into irregular plaques. The slender 3/4 to 1½ inch acorns were an important food source of the California Coastal Indians who ground the acorn meat into a flour which was leeched, then used to make tortilla-like cakes, or soup. This tree is less drought resistant than other oaks here and is found mostly near streams.

☐ **VALLEY OAK** .CATKINS
Quercus lobata   March-April
FOOTHILL WOODLAND
A large deciduous oak with 2½ to 4 inch leaves which are rather deeply round-lobed. Upper surface of the leaves is dark green, the lower light green; both surfaces are hairy. Acorns are 1½ to 2½ inches long and shaped like a pointed cartridge shell. The acorn cup is sculptured and knobby. It grows close to water.

47

☐ **BLUE OAK** . . . . **CATKINS**
Quercus Douglasii   April-May
FOOTHILL WOODLAND

The blue-green leaf color, caused by a scaly wax deposit, is the reason for this tree's name. Leaves are 1 to 3 inches long, ½ to 1½ inches wide, round-lobed and very thick. Its acorns are globular with a pointed tip. This tree is extremely drought resistant.

WALNUT FAMILY

☐ **BLACK WALNUT** . . . . **CATKINS**
Juglans Hindsii   April-May
RIPARIAN

A 40 to 75 ft. tree with a single large trunk and pinnately compound leaves having 15 to 19 leaflets 2½ to 5 inches long. Its edible nuts are 1 to 1½ inches in diameter and very hard. These trees occur mostly around old Indian campsites. The only one known at Pinnacles is near the Chalone Creek Bridge.

WILLOW FAMILY

☐ **FREMONT COTTONWOOD** . . . . **INCONSPICUOUS**
Populus Fremontii   March-April
RIPARIAN

A deciduous tree, with whitish ridged bark, which grows as much as 100 ft. tall. Leaves are yellow green and triangular in shape.

☐ **SANDBAR WILLOW** . . . . **INCONSPICUOUS**
Salix Hindsiana   March-May
RIPARIAN

A shrub, or small tree, 6 to 20 ft. high with furrowed gray bark and linear leaves tapering to a point at both ends. Leaves and stems are covered with short, silky, gray fuzz.

☐ **ARROYO WILLOW** . . . . **FUZZY CATKINS**
Salix lasiolepis   February-April
RIPARIAN

A small shrub with smooth bark and yellowish to brown twigs; usually slightly woolly-hairy. Its linear leaves are dark green above, lighter below, and slightly hairy. Flowering parts are in the form of fuzzy catkins.

NETTLE FAMILY

☐ **STINGING NETTLE** . . . . **GREENISH**
Urtica holosericea   June-September
RIPARIAN

An erect herb whose stems and leaves are covered with small stinging hairs. It grows up to 8 ft. and is usually found in open places along streambeds. Leaves are somewhat triangular, 1 to 3 inches long, with serrated edges, and appear to have a coarse, gray, velvety covering. Indians applied the leaves to their skin as a counter irritant for severe pain. They also made a hot brew of the foliage for treatment of rheumatism and/or arthritis.

EVENING PRIMROSE FAMILY

☐ **CALIFORNIA FUCHSIA or MEXICAN BALSAMEA . . . . RED**
Zauschneria californica   August-October
RIPARIAN
A 1 to 3 ft. plant with double funnel-shaped flowers of 4 petals each; the outer part being colored sepals. Its name comes from the buds which resemble fuchsia buds. The long oval leaves were once used either as a wash for cuts and bruises or a decoction for kidney and bladder trouble. It can easily be mistaken for penstemon.

☐ **FAREWELL-TO-SPRING . . . . .LAVENDER to PURPLE**
Clarkia amoena   June-August
CHAPARRAL AND
FOOTHILL WOODLAND
An herbaceous, flowering annual 1 to 3 ft. tall with ½ to 2 inch leaves of a long narrow shape. There are 4 fan-shaped petals on the 1 inch flower which are often dark at the base with even darker splotches at the bottom. All members of this family have a pistil, longer than the anthers, whose tip is divided into an X-shaped stigma.

☐ **GODETIA . . . . PURPLE**
Clarkia purpurea   April-June
FOOTHILL WOODLAND
Similar to the above plant but smaller. Its flower petals are usually more oval and dark purple. The X-shaped stigma is not so deeply divided.

☐ **GODETIA . . . . DARK PURPLE**
Clarkia purpurea quadrivulnera   April-July
FOOTHILL WOODLAND
Almost identical to the preceding plant but 1/3 the size with flowers less than ½ inch across. Seen in dry grass.

☐ **GODETIA . . . . WHITE to PINKISH**
Clarkia epilobioides   March-May
FOOTHILL WOODLAND
A godetia with small ¼ to ½ inch flowers and linear hairy leaves. This inconspicuous 8 to 24 inch plant grows in shaded spots. Indians collected the seeds of all godetias and mixed them with acorns to flavor the resulting meal or flour.

☐ **CLARKIA** . . . . **SALMON-PINK to PURPLE**
Clarkia unguiculata   May-June
FOOTHILL WOODLAND
An unusual flower named for Captain Clark of "Lewis & Clark" fame.
Its petals have a slender limb which abruptly widens at the tip into a
rhombic shape. Each petal is so long it hardly seems related to the other
3 petals. It grows 1 to 2 ft. tall.

☐ **FAIRY FANS** . . . . **LUMINOUS PINK**
Clarkia Breweri   April-May
FOOTHILL WOODLAND
A 5 to 9 inch herb with a few spreading branches. The 4 petals of the
flower have a short narrow basal limb which rapidly expands into a
broad triangular shape with 3 lobes at the tip. The inner lobe is longer
and narrower than the 2 outer lobes.

☐ **EVENING PRIMROSE** . . . . **YELLOW aging to RED**
Oenothera contorta   May-June
FOOTHILL WOODLAND
A 4 to 16 inch herb with 1 or more slender stems having smooth foliage
and tiny flowers. Oval petals are 1/10 inch long, the sepals are turned
back (reflexed), and its leaves are ½ to 1¼ inches long. Its lobed stigma
is prominent.

☐ **EVENING PRIMROSE** . . . . **YELLOW**
Oenothera micrantha   March-May
CHAPARRAL
An herb with several prostrate spreading stems, 8 to 24 inches long,
found growing in disturbed or burned over areas. Stems often show
peeling skin. Tiny 1/10 inch flowers dry to a green color on aging.

☐ **EVENING PRIMROSE** . . . . **YELLOW**
Oenothera bistorta   March-June
CHAPARRAL
Similar to the preceding plant but with more slender red-colored stems.
Flowers bloom only a few at a time in the leaf axils, and petals have a
dark spot at their base.

BUCKTHORN FAMILY

☐ **REDBERRY or BUCKTHORN** . . . . **GREENISH**
Rhamnus crocea   March-April
CHAPARRAL AND
FOOTHILL WOODLAND
A 5-15 ft. shrub with small, spiny-edged, shiny, dark-green oval leaves.
Inconspicuous flowers are one-sexed. Fruit is a bright-red two-seeded
berry. It is easily mistaken for stunted holly-leafed cherry.

50

☑ **BUCKBRUSH or WILD LILAC** . . . . . **WHITE to PALE BLUE**
Ceanothus cuneatus   March-May
not in flower- 4/78 CHAPARRAL
A dominant shrub of this area with spiny-ended branches bearing small thick wedge-shaped leaves with rounded tips. Small flowers are borne in dense flat-topped clusters at branch ends and exude a heavy sweet fragrance. A few plants here have pale blue flowers. Indians gathered the small 3-parted dry fruits and the foliage is a favorite browse of deer.

MISTLETOE FAMILY

☐ **MISTLETOE** . . . . **GREENISH**
Phoradendron flavescens   Year-round
This common parasite has thick oval green leaves, white sticky berries, and prefers oak trees in this area. Its roots enter the cambium, just under the bark, where water and minerals can easily be obtained. Unless the tree is unhealthy, or the plant unusually thick, little harm is done since it makes most of its food by its leaves. Indians chewed the leaves to relieve toothache.

☐ **DWARF MISTLETOE** . . . . **YELLOW-ORANGE**
Arceuthobium campylopodum   Year-around
A succulent looking parasite, with an odd orangish color, which grows on Digger Pines in thick clumps. It has no chlorophyll and trees infected with it ultimately die. Leaves are small scales; the seed is sticky and adheres to other trees when the fruit explodes. Natural fires are probably the way it has been controlled.

BUCKEYE FAMILY

☑ **CALIFORNIA BUCKEYE** . . . . **WHITE**
Aesculus californica   May-June
RIPARIAN
This small, often many-trunked, tree has smooth whitish bark and 5 long-oval pointed leaflets rising from a common point (palmate leaflets). Large spikes of flowers cover the tree in late spring imparting a delicate scent to the air. The flowers seem toxic to bees. No more than 5, usually 1 or 2, flowers per spike bear fruit. Leaves are shed in midsummer to preserve moisture, leaving the fruits in view. The big brown nut serves as food for some wildlife and Indians ate them after leaching out the poisons. Ground and thrown into streams in a pure state, the nut was used to stun and kill fish.

SUMAC FAMILY

☑ **POISON OAK** . . . . **GREENISH**
Rhus diversiloba   April-May
RIPARIAN AND
FOOTHILL WOODLAND
A western cousin of poison-ivy occuring as a bush or vine. It is often found intermingled with other shrubs and trees. The compound leaves

have 3 leaflets which are highly variable in appearance but often resemble oak leaves. Shiny-green summer leaves turn bright-red before being shed in the fall. Small green flowers produce clusters of waxy white berries, relished by many birds. The plant is browsed by deer and livestock. It is only toxic to most humans.

PARSLEY & CARROT FAMILY

☐ **SNAKEROOT** . . . . **YELLOW**
Sanicula crassicaulis   March-May
RIPARIAN AND
FOOTHILL WOODLAND
A perennial single stemmed plant up to 4½ ft. tall with heart-shaped leaves on the bottom and 3-5 palmate lobes on the upper leaves. Flowers are in compound umbels (flat-topped clusters rising from a common point).

☑ **WILD CELERY** . . . . **WHITE**
Apiastrum angustifolium   March-April
FOOTHILL WOODLAND
A 2-50 inch branching annual with finely dissected (celery-like) leaves and flowers in irregular umbels. Its seeds are smooth and heart-shaped with the smell of celery. Usually in dry sandy soils.

☐ **SHEPHERD'S NEEDLE** . . . . **WHITE**
Scandix pecten   April-June
RIPARIAN
This plant grows 6-14 inches high with much branching which spreads widely from the base. Its finely dissected leaves and its stems are covered with stiff bristly hairs. Flowers produce a long, needle-like, barbed seed which gives it its name.

☐ **RATTLESNAKE WEED** . . . . **WHITE**
Daucus pusillus   April-June
RIPARIAN
Leaves of this plant resemble those of a carrot, to which it is closely related, but grow from a height of 2 inches to 3 ft. Small flowers are typical of this group. It was once used for treatment of snake bite and is common in burned areas.

☐ **EULOPHUS** . . . . **WHITE**
Perideridia californica   April-May
RIPARIAN AND
FOOTHILL WOODLAND
An annual plant with a tuberous root, like a potato, and leaves which are 3-pinnately compound with an overall triangular outline. The umbels of flowers are white with a pinkish cast. Its roots were an important food source to the Indians.

☐ **LOVAGE** . . . . **WHITE**
Ligusticum apiifolium   June-July
FOOTHILL WOODLAND
A stout annual growing 2, 3, or even 6 ft. tall with 3-pinnate compound leaves and white to pinkish flowers.

☐ **VELAEA** . . . . **YELLOW**
Tauschia Kelloggii   April-June
FOOTHILL WOODLAND
A stemless perennial arising from a thick, elongated, odorous, yellow taproot. It has oval leaves on long stems (petioles) and its flowers are small rounded balls.

☐ **HOG-FENNEL** . . . . **YELLOW**
Lomatium utriculatum   February-May
CHAPARRAL AND
FOOTHILL WOODLAND
A low-growing plant arising from a thick tap-root to a height of ½-2 ft. with foliage which is purplish below. Leaves are 3-pinnate compound.

☐ **HOG-FENNEL** . . . . **GREENISH-WHITE to PURPLISH**
Lomatium dasycarpum   March-June
CHAPARRAL
A low 1-1½ ft. plant similar to the preceding but with different colored flowers.

☐ **LEPTOTAENIA** . . . . **YELLOW**
Lomatium californicum   April-June
CHAPARRAL AND
FOOTHILL WOODLAND
A perennial plant 1-4½ ft. tall with compound-leaves and leaflets which are 3-cleft and coarsely toothed.

DOGWOOD FAMILY

☐ **BROWN DOGWOOD** . . . . **WHITE**
Cornus glabrata   May-June
RIPARIAN
A shrub or small tree related to flowering dogwood but having less showy small 4-petaled star-shaped flowers in clusters and bearing whitish to bluish berry-like fruit. The opposite leaves are oval and shiny green.

MADDER FAMILY

☐ **WALL GALIUM** . . . . **GREENISH-WHITE**
Galium parisiense   April-August
FOOTHILL WOODLAND
A tiny-stemmed annual ½-1 ft. high with rough, sandpapery, bristle-tipped leaves in whorls of 5-7 at each node. Extremely tiny flowers are borne in small clusters.

☐ **GOOSE GRASS** . . . . **WHITE**
Galium aparine   March-July
CHAPARRAL AND
FOOTHILL WOODLAND
A sprawling annual, 1-3 ft. long, which tends to grow over other plants. Leaves grow in clusters of 6-8 at the stem nodes; the small flowers grow in clusters coming from upper leaves.

☐ **GROUP WEED** . . . . **WHITE**
Galium trifidium   June-August
RIPARIAN
A perennial with 5-18 inch stems that are much-branched and intertangled, 4-angled, and rather smooth. Leaves occur in whorls of 4, 5, or 6 and the flowers in groups of 1-3 in the leaf axils.

☐ **BEDSTRAW** . . . . **YELLOWISH-GREEN**
Galium Nuttallii   March-June
CHAPARRAL AND
FOOTHILL WOODLAND
A climbing vine-like plant, as tall as 5 ft., growing from a woody base. Leaves are grouped in 4's, rough to the touch, elliptical shaped and ½-1 inch long. The 1/12 inch, 4-petaled flowers occur in clusters.

☐ **BEDSTRAW** . . . . **GREENISH-WHITE**
Galium angustifolium   April-June
CHAPARRAL AND
FOOTHILL WOODLAND
An erect shrubby plant 2-5 ft. tall with stiff branches and ½-1 inch linear leaves rough to the touch. Flowers are like the preceding except for color.

HONEYSUCKLE FAMILY

☐ **BLUE ELDERBERRY** . . . . **CREAMY WHITE**
Sambucus mexicana   March-September
RIPARIAN, CHAPARRAL,
FOOTHILL WOODLAND
A large woody shrub, sometimes a tree, with pinnately-compound leaves of oval, toothed-edged leaflets. The tiny flowers occur in flat-topped compound clusters (pannicles) which give rise to bluish colored berries in late summer. Flowers are sometimes dipped in batter and fried while the berries are used to make jelly and wine. The bark contains an emetic; hollow twigs and stems were made into flutes by Indians. This plant grows wherever an abundant source of water is available.

☐ **MORONEL** . . . . **YELLOW**
Lonicera subspicata   June-July
CHAPARRAL
A vine, or evergreen shrub, with elongated 2-lipped flowers and oval

green leaves covered with tiny fuzzy-white hairs on the underside. Fruit is a yellow to reddish elliptical berry.

☐ **PINK HONEYSUCKLE** . . . . WHITE to PINK
Lonicera hispidula April-July
RIPARIAN
A climbing type shrub with smooth oval green leaves, some of which completely encircle the stem (perfoliate). The pink flowers occur in numerous whorls forming loose spikes.

VALERIAN FAMILY

☐ **PLECTRITIS** . . . . PALE PINK
Plectritis macrocera April-May
FOOTHILL WOODLAND
A small annual herb 3-15 inches tall with opposite oval leaves and clusters, or spikes, of tubular flowers with spurs at their base.

PUMPKIN & SQUASH FAMILY

☐ **COMMON MANROOT or WILD CUCUMBER** . . . . . . WHITE
Marah fabaceus February-April
CHAPARRAL, RIPARIAN,
FOOTHILL WOODLAND
A climbing vine with many tendrils and somewhat maple-shaped leaves, lobed like the palm of a hand (palmate). The tiny white star-shaped flowers are in loose branching spikes and are one-sexed. Female flowers make large, globular, spiny, green fruits which contain shiny-brown marble-like seeds. The vine grows over, and all but chokes out, the vegetation in its vicinity. It is a perennial growing from a huge tap-root which is sometimes man-shaped and may weigh over 100 pounds. Seeds were roasted and used for kidney trouble by the Indians, or ground and thrown into streams to stupify fish.

BELLFLOWER FAMILY

☐ **BELLFLOWER** . . . . BLUE
Campanula angustiflora May-June
CHAPARRAL
A tiny 2-6 inch plant rarely found except on recent burns. Its slender stem bears long-oval leaves and tiny, tubular, bell-shaped flowers about 1/12 inch long.

SUNFLOWER FAMILY

☐ **MULE EARS or COMPASS PLANT** . . . . YELLOW
Wyethia helenoides March-July
CHAPARRAL AND
FOOTHILL WOODLAND
Leaves of this plant appear to spring from the ground, are gray-green, about 1 to 2 ft. long, and shaped like the ears of a mule. Big 3 inch flowers have bright yellow outer petals with a large inner area covered

with medium-brown disc flowers. As with many sunflowers, the heads tend to follow the sun.

☐ **TICKSEED** . . . . **YELLOW**
Coreopsis Douglasii   March-April
CHAPARRAL AND
FOOTHILL WOODLAND
A 5 to 14 inch perennial with narrow thread-like leaves, some of which are pinnately lobed. Long-stemmed flower heads are ½ to 1½ inches wide. The ray-flowers (outside petals) are often white-tipped. The name is from the fact its seeds stick to your clothing like ticks.

☐ **TIDY TIPS** . . . . **WHITE and YELLOW**
Layia platyglossa   May-June
CHAPARRAL AND
FOOTHILL WOODLAND
An annual ½ to 1 ft. tall with hairy linear leaves and single flower heads on the ends of long stems. The whole flower is yellow except for the white-tipped outer petals.

☐ **TIDY TIPS** . . . . **WHITE and YELLOW**
Layia hieracioides   April-June
CHAPARRAL AND
FOOTHILL WOODLAND
Similar to the preceding plant but taller, up to 3 ft., with much branched stems bearing several flower heads at a time. Foliage is covered with bristly white hairs and has a pungent smell.

☐ **TARWEED** . . . . **YELLOW**
Madia exigua   May-July
CHAPARRAL AND
FOOTHILL WOODLAND
A low branching annual 4 to 7 inches high with thread-like stems and small linear leaves. The inconspicuous flower heads are only about 1/12 inch across and the whole plant is usually lost in the grass.

☐ **GUMWEED** . . . . **YELLOW**
Madia anomala   May-June
CHAPARRAL AND
FOOTHILL WOODLAND
An erect plant 1 to 2 ft. tall with ½ to 2 inch linear leaves. There are several flower heads, loosely arranged along the vertical stems, with a sulphur-yellow color.

☐ **CHILE TARWEED** . . . . **LIGHT YELLOW**
Madia sativa   May-October
CHAPARRAL AND
FOOTHILL WOODLAND
Similar to the preceding but with its flower-heads in spikes. The plant is robust and even taller than Gumweed. This native of Chile has made a home in California.

☐ **TARWEED** . . . . **WHITE**
Hemizonia congesta   May-October
CHAPARRAL AND
FOOTHILL WOODLAND
An annual 1 to 1½ ft. tall with slightly-hairy narrow leaves. Flower
heads are borne in the leaf axils, are few in number, and have only a
few flowers; each with 7 apparent petals, which are white.

☐ **TARWEED** . . . . **YELLOW**
Hemizonia Lobbii   May-November
CHAPARRAL AND
FOOTHILL WOODLAND
A much branched annual from ½ to 2 ft. tall but usually low. It has
needle-like leaves and is profusely covered with tiny flower heads
having 3 ray and 3 disc flowers each (3 petals). The glandular foliage is
quite odorous.

☑ **GOLDFIELDS** . . . . **BRIGHT YELLOW**
Baeria chrysostoma   March-May
FOOTHILL WOODLAND and OPEN PLACES
A tiny annual plant no more than 6 inches tall with daisy-like flowering
heads 1/3 to ½ inch across located on stem ends. Leaves are short and
thread-like. In spring these flowers are so abundant in the grassy areas
they appear to carpet the fields with a blanket of solid gold.

☐ **BAERIA** . . . . **YELLOW**
Baeria micorglossa   March-May
FOOTHILL WOODLAND
Very much like the preceding plant but its flowers are only 1/12 inch
across and not so daisy-like. It grows with the other but is not
conspicuous

☐ **GOLDEN YARROW** . . . . **YELLOW**
Eriophyllum confertiflorum   April-August
CHAPARRAL, RIPARIAN
AND FOOTHILL WOODLAND
A 1 to 2 ft. shrub with numerous stems coming from a woody base
with deeply 5-lobed leaves which are pale-green in color and quite
woolly. Flower clusters resemble yarrow but are yellow. Individual
flower heads are only ¼ inch across.

☐ **WIREWEED** . . . . **YELLOW**
Rigiopappus leptocladus   April-June
CHAPARRAL AND
FOOTHILL WOODLAND
A small wiry-looking annual with tiny dandelion-like flowers about 1/3
inch across which are yellow streaked with red. Mature flowers produce
miniature, fluffy, dandelion-like puff balls. Thread-like leaves on the
long wiry stems cause it to be seldom noticed.

☐ SNAKEWEED or MATCHWEED . . . . YELLOW
Gutierrezia Sarothrae May-October
CHAPARRAL
A bushy plant, 1 to 2 ft. tall, with numerous erect wiry stems coming
from a woody base and having thin thread-like leaves. Individual flower
heads are 1/8 inch across and quite numerous on the ends of the
branching stems.

☐ GOLDEN ASTER . . . . YELLOW
Chrysopsis villosa July-October
CHAPARRAL AND
FOOTHILL WOODLAND
A branching herb rising from a perennial woody base with ½ to 1½ inch
oblong leaves covered with tiny glandular hairs. Flower heads occur in
groups of tightly closed clusters at the branch ends.

☐ CALIFORNIA GOLDENROD . . . . YELLOW
Solidago californica July-October
CHAPARRAL AND
FOOTHILL WOODLAND
An erect 2 to 4 ft. plant with numerous oval fine-toothed leaves and
compact terminal flower-clusters in the shape of a pyramid. Individual
flowers are 1/6 to ¼ inch wide.

☐ FLEABANE or WILD DAISY . . . . LIGHT PURPLE with
YELLOW CENTER
Erigeron foliosus May-June
FOOTHILL WOODLAND
A simple erect-branching plant 1 to 2 ft. high with elongated thread-like
leaves and 1 inch flower-heads occuring in clusters on the ends of
branches.

☐ LESSINGIA . . . . YELLOW
Lessingia germanorum August-November
FOOTHILL WOODLAND
An erect woolly plant 4 to 18 inches high with basal and stem leaves
more or less lobed and oblong-shaped. Small flower heads occur singly
on ends of the flower stalk and have 20 to 25 ray and disc-flowers.

☐ MULE FAT . . . . WHITE
Baccharis viminea March-July
RIPARIAN
A tall woody shrub with long, toothed, willow-like leaves and small
white bristly flowers in vase-like pods.

☐ COYOTE BRUSH or CHAPARRAL BROOM . . . . WHITE
Baccharis pilularis   August-December
RIPARIAN
The flowers of this low woody shrub are very much like those of Mule Fat but its bright green foliage has small ½ to 1 inch leaves which are toothed and resemble the shape of scrub-oak leaves.

☐ COMMON YARROW or QUEEN ANN'S LACE . . . . . . WHITE
Achillea lanulosa   June-August
RIPARIAN AND
FOOTHILL WOODLAND
Common throughout most of North America. First a cluster of highly dissected feathery or fern-like leaves of a whitish color appear. Then a 1 to 2 ft. flowering stalk rises from the middle of these leaves and terminates in a rather large flat-topped cluster of tiny white flower heads, the overall effect being that of a piece of lace. From ancient times this plant has been used for medicinal purposes. A brew of leaves in hot water applied to cuts and bruises has a healing effect; crushed fresh plants directly applied to wounds promote blood clotting; so say herbal doctors.

☐ PINEAPPLE WEED . . . . .YELLOW to GREEN
Matricaria matricarioides   May-August
WASTE-PLACES
A lowly herbaceous sweet-smelling plant standing 2 to 10 inches tall and often occuring in large numbers in waste-places. Its common name comes from the flower head which does resemble a pineapple in shape but is only about ¼ inch in diameter and 5/16 inch high. The dried flowers make "chamomile tea."

☐ CALIFORNIA SAGEBRUSH . . . . .GRAYISH
Artemisia californica   August-December
CHAPARRAL
A densely-bushy, gray-green, woody-based shrub 2 to 5 ft. high. Leaves are deeply divided into long thread-like filaments, somewhat lobed at times, and arranged like the palm of your hand (palmately). Flowers are an inconspicuous gray color, resembling little balls, arranged in clusters along a loose spike.

☐ TARRAGON . . . . .GREEN
Artemisia dracunculus   August-October
RIPARIAN
An erect plant of slender stems 2 to 4½ ft. tall with mostly long narrow leaves of dark green color. Lower leaves are sometimes split into 3 parts at the ends. Flower heads are small, green, drooping balls occuring in clusters along stem tops. Unlike most members of the artemisia group, this plant has no distinct smell.

☐ CALIFORNIA MUGWORT . . . . GREEN
Artemisia Douglasiana June-October
RIPARIAN
An aromatic sweet-smelling plant 3-6 ft. tall with leafy stems rising
from a running rootstalk. Most leaves are 2-6 inches wide, 3-5 lobed,
with a whitish underside, and green top. Flowers are small green balls
on the stem ends. Leaves were used to make a tea for colds, colic,
rheumatism, and fever. The leaf juice was supposed to help poison oak.

☐ CREEK SENECIO . . . . YELLOW
Senecio Douglasii June-October
RIPARIAN
A branching bush 2-6 ft. high with narrow, thready, compound leaves
1-3 inches long. It has terminal clusters of flower heads, each head
being about ½ inch wide and producing a white fluffy ball upon
maturing.

☐ GROUNDSEL . . . . YELLOW
Senecio Breweri April-June
CHAPARRAL
A perennial plant with a stout tap-root from the top of which most of
the leaves rise near the ground. Leaves are 7-9 inches long with 1-9 pairs
of lobes. The ½ inch flower heads occur in clusters at the top of 1-2½
ft. nearly leafless stems.

☐ COMMON GROUNDSEL . . . . YELLOW
Senecio vulgaris Year-round
CHAPARRAL, RIPARIAN
AND FOOTHILL WOODLAND
A 6-12 inch plant with simple or branching stems bearing
irregularly-lobed, jagged-edged leaves. Flower heads are cylindrical in
shape with tightly bunched, petal-like ray flowers. When mature, they
open into white fluff-balls.

☐ CUDWEED or COTTON BATTING . . . . . GREENISH WHITE
Gnaphalium chilense June-October
CHAPARRAL AND
FOOTHILL WOODLAND
A whitish herb covered with fuzzy white hairs. It grows from ½-2½ ft.
tall and is often densely clothed with long narrow leaves. Round
globular flower heads are covered with stiff whitish hairs and occur in
clusters at ends of branches.

☐ PEARLY EVERLASTING . . . . YELLOWISH
Anaphalis margaritacea June-August
CHAPARRAL AND
FOOTHILL WOODLAND
An herb with 1-2 ft. simple stems rising from a common root. Its 2-5
inch narrowly oblong leaves are curled under at their edges and have a
lemon-like odor. Flower heads occur in clusters at stem ends and, after
maturing, their bracts dry to a pearly-white which lasts indefinitely.

☐ **FLUFFWEED** . . . . **WHITE**
   Filago gallica   April-June
CHAPARRAL AND
FOOTHILL WOODLAND
A low woolly-white herb 5-7 inches tall having narrow ½-1 inch leaves
with pointed tips. Flower heads are round balls borne in scattered
clusters of 1-6 from the base to the top of the plant.

☐ **MICROPIS** . . . . **WHITISH**
   Micropis californicus   April-June
FOOTHILL WOODLAND
A thin wiry woolly-white herb with a single 4-13 inch stem. The woolly
narrowly-oblong leaves are pointed at the tip and flower clusters are
small fluffy balls about the size of a BB.

☐ **COBWEB THISTLE** . . . . **RED**
   Cirsium occidentale   April-July
FOOTHILL WOODLAND
A 3 ft. perennial thistle rising from a thick taproot with 2-10 inch
pinnately lobed leaves bearing prickled edges. Bright-red flower-heads
are about 2 inches across and surrounded by cupped receptacles of
prickly bracts. Looking straight down into the flower you see long
filamentous hairs arranged in a circular pattern resembling cobwebs.
Indians used the fibers of this plant for weaving and making ropes.

☐ **NAPA THISTLE or TOCALOTE** . . . . **YELLOW**
   Centaurea melitensis   May-June
CHAPARRAL AND
FOOTHILL WOODLAND
An erect annual which does not branch from the base and grows to 2 ft.
tall. Its leaves spring directly from the stem, the lower portion being so
close the stem appears winged. Flower heads issue forth from a spiny
globular receptacle as small yellow tufts. The receptacle thorns are 1/3
to 1/6 inch long.

☐ **STAR THISTLE or BARNABY'S THISTLE** . **BRIGHT YELLOW**
   Centaurea solstitialis   May-October
FOOTHILL WOODLAND
An annual which is diffusely branched at the base and covered with
cottony hairs. It rarely exceeds 12 inches in height with leaves similar
to the preceding plant but much narrower. Flower heads are borne
singly at the branch ends and are expanded into a bright yellow puff
from a globular receptacle having long, ½-¾ inch spines.

☐ **MOUNTAIN DANDELION** . . . . **YELLOW**
   Agoseris heterophylla   April-July
FOOTHILL WOODLAND
A 3-12 inch herb with long narrow leaves appearing to rise directly
from the root. Flower heads are borne singly on long hollow stems and
resemble common dandelions both in fruit and flower.

☐ **LARGE-LEAF MOUNTAIN DANDELION** . . . . **YELLOW**
Agoseris grandiflora   May-July
FOOTHILL WOODLAND
This large stout dandelion-like plant grows to 2¼ ft. from a thick taproot. The oblong leaves are a foot, or more, in length and slightly lobed. The 1-1½ inch flower heads occur singly at the ends of tall hollow stems; a giant-sized edition of the preceding plant.

☐ **CHICORY** . . . . **PINK**
Stephanomeria virgata   July-October
CHAPARRAL AND
FOOTHILL WOODLAND
A wiry stout plant with a thick central stem up to 4 ft. tall. Its slender thin leaves are 1½-6 inches long and its ¼ inch flowers are borne in broad terminal clusters of 4-22 individual flower heads.

☐ **MALACOTHRIX** . . . . **YELLOW**
Malacothrix Clevelandii   April-June
CHAPARRAL
A 5-16 inch herb with a basal whorl of narrow, slightly lobed, 1-3 inch leaves and a much-branched flowering stem having many ¼ inch dandelion-like flowers.

☐ **SMOOTH CATS-EAR** . . . . **YELLOW**
Hypochoeris glabra   March-June
CHAPARRAL
AND RIPARIAN
A small herb 4-16 inches tall with a basal whorl of oblong-oval leaves and tall naked flower-stalks with terminal clusters of ¾ inch flowers resembling their close relative, the dandelion.

☐ **PRICKLY LETTUCE** . . . . **YELLOW**
Lactuca serriola   May-September
CHAPARRAL, RIPARIAN
AND FOOTHILL WOODLAND
This large leafy native of Europe is a true lettuce. It grows 2-5 ft. tall with big hollow stems and 2-3 inch leaves which are spiny-toothed with a row of prickles on the underside of the midrib. There are 9-14 cylindrically shaped flower heads occurring in a cluster at the top of the stem.

☐ **CHAMOMILE or DOG FENNEL** . . . . . **WHITE PETALS with**
YELLOW CENTERS
Anthemis cotula   April-August
CHAPARRAL, RIPARIAN
AND FOOTHILL WOODLAND
An annual up to 3 ft. tall with 3/4-1 inch daisy-like blooms. The finely dissected 1 inch leaves resemble carrot leaves. Its conical seeds are covered with short knobs and stick to your clothing.

(MONOCOTS)

LILY FAMILY

☐ **SOAP PLANT or AMOLE** . . . . **WHITE**
   Chlorogallum pomeridianum   May-August
                        CHAPARRAL AND
                        FOOTHILL WOODLAND
The leaves of this plant rise from a 1-4 inch bulb, covered with brown
fibrous material, and are about 1 inch wide and 8-28 inches long with
wavy edges. The flowering stalk grows to 5 ft., is sparingly branched,
and bears its flowers in loose clusters on the ends of the branches. The
flower has 3 petals and 3 sepals, which look alike, and blooms after
sundown so is not conspicuous in the daytime. The bulb was ground to
make a soapy lather for washing as well as to spread on water to stun
fish.

☐ **DEATH CAMAS** . . . . **WHITE**
   Zigadenus venenosus   May-July
                        FOOTHILL WOODLAND
Its long, narrow leaves measure 6-12 inches by ½ inch wide and rise
from a 1½-1 inch bulb. The 1-3½ ft. flower stalks bear elongated
clusters of tiny star-shaped flowers of 3 petals and 3 sepals, identical in
appearance to each other, which measure about 1/3 inch across. This
plant is poisonous to livestock and humans. The bulbs were crushed to
make a poultice for the treatment of sores, rheumatism, and snake-bite.

☐ **STAR LILY** . . . . **WHITE**
   Zigadenus Fremontii   March-May
                        CHAPARRAL AND
                        FOOTHILL WOODLAND
Similar to, but somewhat larger than, the preceding lily. It grows to 2½
ft., its bulb is 1½-3 inches wide, its greenish-yellow leaves are 8-24
inches by 3/4 inch wide, and its flowers ½-1 inch across with star-shape
and ivory color.

☐ **MARIPOSA LILY** . . . . **WHITE with DARK-RED SPOTS**
   Calochortus venustus   May-July
                        FOOTHILL WOODLAND
A large ivory to pinkish bell-shaped flower about 1½ inches across with
dark red spots on the inside of the petals. Flowers occur on long 1 ft.
stalks and are usually single; sometimes there are up to 3 blooms on one
stalk. The few leaves are small, long, narrow, and cluster around the
plant base. Its bulbs have been an important food source to many.

63

AGAVE FAMILY

☐ **YUCCA or OUR LORD'S CANDLE** . . . . **WHITE**
Yucca Whipplei   April-May
CHAPARRAL AND
FOOTHILL WOODLAND
Until it flowers, this plant consists of a basal rosette of thick
sharp-pointed gray-green leaves from 1-2½ ft. long and varying from a 3
inch width at their base to 1 inch along most of their length. The plant
blooms only once. It sends up a large thick asparagus-like stalk to a
height of 8-14 ft. and bears a large tapering spike of 1-inch bell-shaped
flowers about 3 ft. long. The flower is pollinated by a small white
"Yucca Moth." Where the moth does not occur the yucca makes little
or no fruit. Indians used the leaf fibers for making twine and rope and
roasted the roots for a potato-like food.

CAT-TAIL FAMILY

☐ **CAT-TAIL or BLUE FLAG** . . . . **BLUISH-GREEN**
Typha glauca   June
RIPARIAN
This 6-10 ft. rush-like plant grows in the water from a creeping
root-stalk or rhizome. Foliage is bluish-green as are the early flowers
which are borne in very tight spikes, the upper consisting of male
flowers and the lower portion female flowers. When flowers mature and
dry, the familiar cat-tail is produced.

AMARYLLIS FAMILY

☐ **MEXICALLI ONION** . . . . **RED to PURPLE**
Allium peninsulare   March-June
FOOTHILL WOODLAND
A wild onion with 2-4 onion-like leaves from 8-16 inches long with a
flower stem about the same length ending in a compact cluster of 1/3-½
inch flowers all rising from the same point on the flower stem. Indians
rubbed the crushed leaves on their skin for insect repellent and ate the
bulbs.

☐ **PURPLE WILD ONION or DWARF ONION** . . . **ROSE-PURPLE**
Allium fimbriatum   March-July
CHAPARRAL
AND XERIC
A dwarf onion about 2-3 inches high with clusters of rose-purple
flowers. Each is 6-petaled with dark mid-veins; the cluster being about
the same size as the preceding plant.

☐ **WILD ONION** . . . . **WHITE to PINKISH**
Allium amplectens   March-June
FOOTHILL WOODLAND
A wild onion with 8-20 inch flower-stalks bearing white to pinkish
flowers about 2/3 inches across. Thin rounded leaves are shorter than
the flower stalks.

☐ **WILD ONION**. . . . . **WHITE to PINKISH**
Allium lacunosum   April-May
FOOTHILL WOODLAND
A wild onion similar to the preceding but 4-8 inches high with the
flower petals having a prominent mid-vein which is green or red. Thin
rounded leaves are as long as the flowering stem.

☐ **GOLDEN STARS or BLOOMERIA** . . . . **YELLOW**
Bloomeria crocea   April-June
FOOTHILL WOODLAND
A prominent plant with 6-petaled, star-shaped, orange-yellow flowers
growing from a common point on a single flowering stem ½-1½ ft. tall.
Each petal has a dark-brownish center line. Long linear leaves occur at
the base of the plant but are not usually noticed.

☑ **GOLDEN BRODIAEA** . . . . **YELLOW**
Brodiaea lutea   May August
CHAPARRAL AND
FOOTHILL WOODLAND
Very similar, but later blooming, to the preceding plant and often
confused with it. Flowers are a lighter, or brighter, yellow and the dark
streak along the mid-line of the petals is not as pronounced, or absent.

☐ **HARVEST BRODIAEA** . . . . **BLUE to PURPLE**
Brodiaea cornnaria   May-July
FOOTHILL WOODLAND
The flowering stems of this plant range from 7-20 inches high and bear
broad open clusters of 6-petaled light-blue to purple flowers with each
on a distinct stem of its own. Long narrow leaves are usually dry by
blooming time and not visible.

☑ **BLUE DICKS or WILD HYACINTH** . . . . . . **BLUE to PURPLE**
Brodiaea pulchella   March-May
FOOTHILL WOODLAND
This plant has 1-3 ft. flowering stems and, like Harvest Brodiaea, no
visible leaves at blooming time. The flowers, similar but darker, have
almost no individual stems.

RUSH FAMILY
☐ **BOG RUSH** . . . . **NOT CONSPICUOUS**
Juncus effusus   June-August
RIPARIAN
A common 2-4 ft. rush with round stems and many clusters of minute,
brownish, dried-looking flowers. It grows in dense clumps.

☐ **WIRE RUSH** . . . . **GREENISH**
Juncus balticus   May-August
RIPARIAN
These grass-like plants stand 1-3½ ft. high, have rounded stems, and many clusters of minute greenish flowers, sometimes tinged with purple.

☐ **IRIS RUSH** . . . . **NOT CONSPICUOUS**
Juncus xiphioides   May-October
RIPARIAN
The stems of this plant are not so round as the others but are considerably flattened and stand 1½-3 ft. high. Leaves surrounding the stem bear a strong resemblance to those of an iris plant.

SEDGE FAMILY

☐ **UMBRELLA SEDGE** . . . . **NOT CONSPICUOUS**
Cyperus strigosus   July-October
RIPARIAN
A 1-3 ft. sedge of grass-like leaves with a typical triangular cross-section and somewhat rough. It has large flat-topped clusters of triangular flower spikes surrounded at the base by 3 leaf-like bracts. Flower spikelets are somewhat flattened. The root is a rhizome.

☐ **SEDGE** . . . .**NO FLOWER PETALS**
Carex nebraskensis   Year-round
RIPARIAN
A sedge growing in clumps; the flowering stems are 10-48 inches high and bear thin 1-1½ inch spikes of all male or female flowers which arise from the same stem. Female spikes are broader and lower on the stem, which is triangular in cross-section.

☐ **SPIKE RUSH** . . . .**INCONSPICUOUS**
Helocharis sp.   May-September
RIPARIAN
These may be 2 species; 1 tall and 1 short. Unlike most sedges, their stems tend to be oval to round in cross-section. Leaves are so reduced they are not apparent and flowers are borne in small, terminal spikes at stem tips, though some stems are barren.

☐ **PANICLE BULRUSH** . . . .**INCONSPICUOUS**
Scirpus microcarpus   May-August
RIPARIAN
A 2-5 ft. sedge with triangular leafy stems. Leaves are long, narrow and rough to the touch. Greenish flower-spikes occur in small clusters of 2-5 which are part of a larger flat-topped arrangement of these small clusters.

☐ **CALIFORNIA BULRUSH** . . . . .INCONSPICUOUS
Scirpus californicus   June-September
RIPARIAN
Taller, 3-9 ft., but similar to the preceding species, with dark red-brown
spikelets arranged in broad terminal clusters.

GRASS FAMILY

☐ **SOFT CHESS or SOFT CHEAT**
Bromus mollis   April-July
CHAPARRAL AND
FOOTHILL WOODLAND
A tufted annual grass from 8-24 inches tall with 2-4 inch wide
soft-hairy leaf-blades and stiff, dense, erect fruiting-heads from 2-4
inches long.

☐ **RIPGUT GRASS**
Bromus rigidus   April-June
FOOTHILL WOODLAND
This annual grass, a native of Europe, stands about 8-28 inches tall with
coarsly hairy leaf-blades and dense, drooping, fruiting heads consisting
of a few spikelets 3-6 inches long. Long barbed awns of the seeds
penetrate the skin of livestock around mouth, nose and eyes causing
sores and blindness. It can also penetrate the intestines; hence the
name.

☐ **RED BROME or FOXTAIL CHESS**
Bromus rubens   March-June
FOOTHILL WOODLAND
This grass is similar to the preceding two but grows only 6-16 inches
high. Erect bushy fruiting-heads resemble ragged bristled-brushes and
have a red color to them. This Brome grass and the first two Brome
grasses are all natives of Europe and all potentially harmful to livestock.

☐ **FOXTAIL FESCUE**
Festuca megalura   April-June
FOOTHILL WOODLAND
A tufted annual grass 8-24 inches tall with smooth leaf-blades and
narrow fruiting heads, which are somewhat 1-sided, measuring 2½-8
inches in length. Awns of its seed are long and rough.

☐ **ANNUAL BLUEGRASS**
Poa annua   January-July
WASTE PLACES
A small light-green grass less than 8 inches tall, matted, weak, and
spreading by runners with flattened stems and pyramid shaped fruiting
heads 1-2½ inches long. Fruiting heads have short spreading branches
and 3-6 flowered spikelets. This native of Europe grows alongside roads
and in waste places.

☐ GOLDENTOP
Lamarkia aurea   February-May
CHAPARRAL
This short erect annual seldom exceeds 4 inches here but may grow to
12 inches elsewhere. The fruiting head is its distinguishing characteristic
in that it occupies ½ the stem length and all the seeds are borne on 1
side of the stem, giving the appearance of a miniature rat-tail comb.
When mature, this native of the Mediterranean turns a golden shiny
color and persists throughout the summer along the trailsides.

☐ CALIFORNIA MELIC
Melica californica   April-May
FOOTHILL WOODLAND
An annual grass 2 to 4½ ft. tall with stems issuing from a bulbous
corm-like swelling just above the roots. The grass blades start at this
swelling, which is their base, and narrow to a width of 1 to 2 inches.
Fruiting heads are long, narrow and dense packed with small spikelets
of 2 to 5 flowers.

☐ TORREY MELIC
Melica torreyana   March-June
RIPARIAN AND
FOOTHILL WOODLAND
A weak slender-stemmed grass 12-40 inches tall with narrow blades and
broadly spreading fruiting heads from 3-10 inches long. The parts of
spikelets making up these heads are quite hairy.

☐ SILVER HAIRGRASS
Aira caryophyllea   April-June
WASTE PLACES
Small tufts of grass 4-12 inches high with the fruiting-head stems widely
branched, resembling miniature trees with open crowns. Spikelets are a
shiny-silvery color. Introduced from Europe, you find it on open dry
ground throughout the monument.

☐ WILD OAT
Avena fatua   April-June
WASTE PLACES
A familiar common grass having stems 1-4 ft. tall bearing large open
fruiting heads which appear quite bristly or hairy due to the long awns
of the seeds. This native of Europe is closely related to cultivated oats
and was used as food by the Indians after it was introduced to this
country.

☐ BEARD GRASS or RABBIT FOOT GRASS
Polypogon monspeliensis   April-August
RIPARIAN
An annual 6-20 inches tall with dense soft-silky fruiting heads occuring
singly on the ends of stems in an upright position. The silky texture
comes from its long awns. It is another native of Europe.

☐ **NIT GRASS**
Gastridium ventricosum   May-September
                    WASTE PLACES
A shallow rooted grass growing 8-25 inches high with dense
cigar-shaped spike-like fruiting heads borne singly on each stem in an
upright position with silvery or yellowish spikelets. This is another
native of Europe.

INDEX

Achillea lanulosa 59
Adiantim Jordani 21
Adenostoma fasciculatum 44
Aesculus californica 51
Agoseris heterophylla 61
        grandiflora 62
Aira caryophylea 68
Allium amplectens 65
        fimbriatum 64
        lacunosum 65
        peninsulare 64
AMOLE 63
Amsinckia Douglasiana 36
        intermedia 36
Anagallis arvensis 30
Anaphalis Margaritacea 60
Anthemis cotula 62
Anthirrhinum Kellogii 39
        multiflorum 39
        vexillo 39
Apiastrum angustifolium 52
Arabis Breweri 27
Arceuthobium campylopodum 51
Arctostaphylos glauca 31
        pungens 30
Arenaria Douglasii 27
Artemisia californica 59
        Douglasiana 60
        dracunculus 59
Asclepias fascicularis 31
ASH, FLOWERING 31
ASTER, GOLDEN 58
Avena fatua 68
BABY BLUE EYES 34
Baccharis viminea 58
        pilularis 59
BAERIA 57
Baeria chrysostoma 57
        microglossa 57
Barbarea vulgaris 26
BEARD GRASS 68
BEARD-TONGUE, VIOLET 38
BEDSTRAW 54
BEE PLANT, CALIFORNIA 39
BELLFLOWER 55
BIRDSFOOT TREFOIL 56
BITTERROOT 27
BLACKBERRY 44
BLOOMERIA 65
Bloomeria crocea 65
BLUE DICKS 65
BLUE FLAG 64
BLUEGRASS, ANNUAL 67

BLUE SKULLCAP 40
Brassica campestris 26
BREWER'S ROCKCRESS 27
BRODIAEA, GOLDEN 65
        HARVEST 65
Brodiaea coronaria 65
        lutea 65
        pulchella 65
Bromus mollis 67
        rigidus 67
        rubens 67
BROOM, CHAPARRAL 59
BROOMRAPE 40
BUCKBRUSH 51
BUCKEYE, CALIFORNIA 51
BUCKTHORN 50
BUCKWHEAT, CALIFORNIA 29
BULRUSH, CALIFORNIA 67
        PANICLED 66
BUR CLOVER 46
BUTTERCUP, CALIFORNIA 23
Calandrinia ciliata 28
CALIFORNIA BEE PLANT 39
        BROOM 47
        BUCKEYE 51
        BULRUSH 67
        BUTTERCUP 23
        FUCHSIA 49
        GOLDENROD 58
        HOLLY 45
        MAIDENHAIR
            FERN 21
        MELIC 68
        MUGWORT 59
        POPPY 25
        SAGEBRUSH 59
        SAXIFRAGE 42
Calochortus venustus 63
Campanula angustiflora 55
CAMPHOR WEED 40
Carex nebraskensis 66
Castilleja affinis 40
        foliolosa 40
CAT-TAIL 64
CAT'S EAR, SMOOTH 62
Ceanothus cuneatus 51
CELERY, WILD 52
Centaurea melitensis 61
        solstitialis 61
Centaurium exaltatum 31
CENTAU, TALL 31
Cerastium viscosum 27
Cercocarpus betuloides 44

CHAMISE 44
CHAMOMILE 62
CHAPARRAL BROOM 59
    CURRANT 43
    NIGHTSHADE . . .37
    PEA 45
CHEAT, SOFT 67
CHERRY, HOLLY LEAF 44
CHESS, FOXTAIL 67
    SOFT 67
CHIA 41
CHICKWEED, MOUSE-EARED . .27
CHICORY 62
CHINESE HOUSES 39
Chlorogallum pomeridianum 63
Chorizanthe Douglasii 28
    membranacea 28
Chrysopsis villosa 58
Cirsium occidentale 61
CLARKIA 50
Clarkia amoena 49
    Breweri 50
    epilobioides 49
    purpurea 49
    purpurea quadrivulnera . . .49
    unguiculata 50
Clematis lasiantha 23
    ligusticifolia 23
CLIFFBRAKE 20
CLOVER, BUR 46
    OWL 39
CLUBMOSS, LITTLE 20
Collinsia concolor 39
COMPASS PLANT 55
Convolvulus occidentalis 32
    subacaulis 32
Coreopsis Douglasii 56
Cornus glabrata 53
COTTON BATTING 60
COTTONWOOD, FREMONT 48
COYOTE BRUSH 59
CREAM-CUPS 25
CREEK SENECIO 60
CRESS, WINTER 26
Cryptantha muricata 36
CUCUMBER, WILD 55
CUDWEED 60
CURRANT, CHAPARRAL 43
Cuscuta brachycalyx 32
Cyperus strigosus 66
DAISY, WILD 58
DANDELION, LARGE-LEAF
    MOUNTAIN . . .62
    MOUNTAIN 61
Datura meteloides 37
Daucus pusillus 52
DEATH CAMAS 63

DEERWEED 47
Delphinium decorum 22
    Parryi 23
Dendromecon rigida 25
Dentaria californica 26
DESERT OLIVE 31
Dicentra chrysantha 25
DIGGER PINE 22
DOCK, CURLY 30
    WILLOW 29
DODDER 32
Dodecatheon Clevelandii 30
    Hendersonii 30
DOG-FENNEL 62
DOGWOOD, BROWN 53
Dryopteris arguta 21
Dudleya cymosa 42
EAR-DROPS, GOLDEN 25
ELDERBERRY, BLUE 54
ELLISIA 34
Emmenanthe penduliflora 35
Equisetum arvense 20
Eremocarpus setigerus 24
Eriastrum densifolium 33
    virgatum 33
Erigeron foliosus 58
ERIOGONUM 28-29
ERIOGONUM, WHITE-LEAFED . .29
Eriogonum Baileyi 28
    elongatum 29
    fasciculatum 29
    latifolium 29
    Nortonii 29
    saxatile 29
    vimineum 28
Eriodyction californicum 35
    crassifolium 36
    tomentosum 35
Eriophyllum confertiflorum 57
Erodium cicutarium 24
Erysimum capitatum 27
Eschscholzia californica 25
Eucrypta chrysanthemumifolia . . .34
EULOPHUS 52
Euphorbia ocellata 24
EVENING PRIMROSE 50
EVENING SNOW 33
FAIRY FANS 50
FALSE MALLOW 23
FAMILY, AGAVE 63
    AMARYLLIS 64
    BELLFLOWER 55
    BROOMRAPE 40
    BUCKEYE 51
    BUCKTHORN 50
    BUCKWHEAT 28
    BUTTERCUP 22

71

FAMILY, CARROT 52
     CAT-TAIL..........64
     DODDER 32
     DOGWOOD 53
     EVENING PRIMROSE .49
     FERN 20
     FORGET-ME-NOT 36
     FUMITORY 25
     GENTIAN..........31
     GERANIUM 24
     GOOSEBERRY 42
     GRASS 67
     HEATH............30
     HONEYSUCKLE 54
     HORSETAIL........20
     JUNIPER...........22
     LILY 63
     LOASA 24
     MADDER 53
     MALLOW 23
     MILKWEED 31
     MINT 40
     MISTLETOE........51
     MORNING-GLORY....32
     MOSS-ROSE 27
     MUSTARD 25
     NETTLE 48
     NIGHTSHADE 37
     OAK 47
     OLIVE............31
     PEA.............45
     PHLOX 32
     PINE 22
     PINK 27
     PLANTAIN........30
     POPPY 25
     PRIMROSE 30
     ROSE 43
     RUSH 65
     SEDGE 66
     SNAPDRAGON......37
     SPIKEMOSS 20
     SPURGE 24
     SQUASH 55
     STONECROP 42
     SUMAC...........51
     SUNFLOWER 55
     SYCAMORE 47
     VALERIAN.........55
     VIOLET 24
     WALNUT 48
     WATERLEAF 34
     WILLOW 48
FARE-WELL-TO-SPRING......49
FENNEL, DOG 62
     HOG 53
FERN, BIRD'S FOOT 20

FERN, BRACKEN............20
     CHAIN 21
     COFFEE 20
     GOLDBACK 21
     LICORICE.............21
     MAIDENHAIR 21
     SHIELD..............21
     WOOD...............21
FESCUE, FOXTAIL 67
Festuca megalura 67
FIDDLENECK................36
FIELD MUSTARD 26
FIESTA FLOWER.............34
Filago gallica 61
FILAREE, RED STEMMED 24
FLAX, PINK 24
FLEABANE 58
FLOWERING ASH 31
FLUFFWEED 61
Forestiera neomexicana.........31
FORGET-ME-NOT, WHITE 36
Fraxinus dipetala..............31
FRINGEPOD.................26
FUCHSIA, CALIFORNIA......49
GALIUM, WALL.............53
Galium angustifolium...........54
     aparine.................54
     Nuttallii 54
     parisiense 53
     trifidium 54
GAPING PENSTEMON 38
Gastridium ventricosum 69
Gilia achillaefolia 32
     capitata 32
GILIA 33
GILIA, DWARF..............32
     GLOBE 32
     PRICKLY 33
     STICKY PRICKLY 33
     YELLOW..............32
Gnaphalium chilense 60
GODETIA 49
GOLDEN EAR-DROPS 25
GOLDEN STARS.............65
GOLDENROD, CALIFORNIA ...58
GOLDENTOP 68
GOLDFIELDS 57
GOOSEBERRY, HILLSIDE......43
     SPINY........43
GOOSE GRASS...............54
GRASS, ANNUAL BLUE 67
     BEARD 68
     GOOSE 54
     NIT 69
     RABBIT FOOT 68
     RIPGUT.............67
     SOFT CHEAT 67

GRASS, SOFT CHESS.........67
GREASEWOOD..............44
GROUNDSEL...............60
      COMMON......60
GROUPWEED...............54
GUMWEED.................56
Gutierrezia Sarothrae..........58
HAIRGRASS, SILVER........68
HEDGENETTLE.............41
HELIOTROPE, WILD..........35
Helocharis sp.................66
Hemizonia congesta...........57
      Lobbii............57
Heteromeles arbutifolia........45
HOG-FENNEL................53
HOLLY, CALIFORNIA.......45
HOLLY-LEAF CHERRY.......44
HONEYSUCKLE (MORONEL)...54
HONEYSUCKLE, PINK.......55
HOREHOUND, COMMON......41
HORSETAIL.................20
HYACINTH, WILD...........65
Hypochoeris glabra.............62
INDIAN PAINTBRUSH.......40
      WOOLLY.40
INDIAN WARRIOR...........39
JEWEL FLOWER.............26
JOHNNY JUMP-UP...........24
Juglans Hindsii.................48
Juncus balticus.................66
     effusus...............65
     xiphioides.............66
JUNIPER, UTAH.............22
Juniperus osteosperma.........22
Lactuca serriola...............62
Lamarkia aurea...............68
LARKSPUR................22-23
Lathyrus laetiflorus............47
Layia hieracioides..............56
     platyglossa..............56
Lepechinia calycina............41
Lepidium nitidum..............26
LEPTOTAENIA...............53
LESSINGIA..................58
Lessingia germanorum.........58
LETTUCE, MINER'S.........28
      PRICKLY..........62
      ROCK............42
Lewisia rediviva...............27
Ligusticum apiifolium...........53
LILAC, WILD................57
LILY, MARIPOSA............63
    STAR...............63
LINANTHUS................34
LINANTHUS, PIGMY.........33
Linanthus androsaceus.........34
     ciliatus..............34

Linanthus dichotomus..........33
     pygmaeus............33
Linum micranthum.............24
Lithophragma affinis...........43
     heterophylla......43
LIVE-FOREVER.............42
Lonicera hispidula............55
     subspicata............54
Lomatium californicum........53
     dasycarpum.........53
     utriculatum..........53
LOTUS....................46
LOTUS, HILL...............46
Lotus humistratus.............46
     micranthus.............46
     salsuginosus............46
     scoparius...............47
     subpinnatus.............46
LOVAGE...................53
LUPINE....................15
      HOLLOW-LEAF......45
      SPOTTED BLUE......46
      WHITE-LEAVED BUSH.46
      WHITE-VEINED......45
Lupinus albifrons..............46
     concinnus.............45
     densiflorus.............45
     micranthus............46
     subvexus..............45
     succulentus............45
Madia anomala...............56
     exigua................56
     sativa................56
Malacothamnus Abbottii.......23
MALACOTHRIX.............62
Malacothrix Clevelandii.........62
MALLOW, FALSE............23
MANROOT, COMMON........55
MANZANITA, BIG-BERRY.....31
      MEXICAN......30
Marah fabaceus...............55
Marrubium vulgare............41
MATCHWEED...............58
Matricaria matricarioides........59
Medicago hispida..............46
Melica californica.............68
     torreyanna.............68
MENTZELIA................24
Mentzelia gracilenta...........24
MEXICAN BALSAMEA........49
MICROPUS.................61
Micropus californicus..........61
MICROSTERIS..............32
Microsteris gracilis............32
MILKWEED, MEXICAN.......31
Mimulus auranticus............38
     cardinalis............37

73

Mimulus floribundus 37
     Fremontii 38
     guttatus 38
     Rattanii 38
MINT, COYOTE 42
MISTLETOE 51
     DWARF 51
Monardella villosa 42
MONKEY FLOWER,
     CHAPARRAL. . .38
     COMMON
     YELLOW . .38
     DESERT 38
     SCARLET. . . .37
     STICKY 38
     YELLOW 37
Montia perfoliata 28
MORNING GLORY, COMMON . .32
     PURPLE RIBBED . .32
MORONEL 54
MOUNTAIN MAHOGANY 44
MUGWORT, CALIFORNIA 59
MULE EARS 55
MULE FAT 58
MULLEIN, TURKEY. 24
MUSTARD, FIELD 26
Nasturtium officinale 26
Navarretia actractyloides 33
     mitracarpa 33
NEMOPHILA, WHITE 34
Nemophila Menziesii 34
Nicotiana attenuata 37
     Bigelovii 37
NIGHTSHADE, CHAPARRAL . . .37
OAK, BLUE. 48
     COAST LIVE. 47
     POISON 51
     VALLEY 47
OAT, WILD 68
Oenothera bistorta 50
     contorta 50
     micrantha 50
OLIVE, DESERT. 31
ONION, DWARF 64
     MEXICALLI 64
     PURPLE WILD 64
     WILD 65
ORPIN 42
Orobanche bulbosa. 40
Orthocarpus purpurascens 39
OUR LORD'S CANDLE 64
OWL CLOVER. 39
PANSY, YELLOW 24
Parvisedum pentandrum 42
PEA, CHAPARRAL. 45
     SAN DIEGO 47
PEARLY EVERLASTING 60

Pedicularis densiflora 39
Pelleae andromedaefolia 20
     mucronata 20
PENSTEMON, GAPING 38
Penstemon breviflorus 38
     centranthifolius 38
     heterophyllus. 38
PEPPERGRASS, COMMON. 26
Perideridia californica. 52
PHACELIA 35
     ROCK 35
     STINGING. 35
Phacelia brachyloba 35
     californica 35
     distans 35
     Rattanii 35
Pholistoma auritum 34
     membranaceum 34
Phoradendron flavescens 51
Pickeringia montana. 45
PIGMY WEED 42
PINE, DIGGER 22
PINEAPPLE WEED 59
PINK FLAX 24
PINK, WINDMILL 27
Pinus sabiniana. 22
PIPESTEM 23
Pityrogramma triangularis 21
Plagiobothrys californica 36
     canescens 36
     nothofulvus. 36
PLANTAIN 30
Plantago Hookeriana 30
Platanus racemosa 47
Platystemon californicus 25
PLECTRITUS 55
Plectritus macrocera. 55
Poa annua 67
POISON OAK 51
Polypodium glycyrrhiza. 21
Polypogon monspeliensis 68
POPCORN FLOWER. 36
POPPY, CALIFORNIA 25
     TREE 25
     WIND 25
Populus Fremontii 48
Potentilla glandulosa 43
POTENTILLA, STICKY. 43
Prunus illicifolia 44
Pteridium aquilinum. 20
QUEEN ANN'S LACE 59
Quercus agrifolia 47
     Douglasii 48
     lobata 47
Ranunculus californicus 23
RATTLESNAKE WEED. 52
REDBERRY. 50
RED BROME 67

RED MAIDS 68
Rhamnus crocea. 50
Rhus diversiloba. 51
Ribes californicum 43
    malvaceum 43
    quercetorum. 43
Rigiopappus leptocladus 57
ROCKCRESS, BREWER'S 27
Rosa californica 44
ROSE, WILD 44
Rubus vitifolius 44
Rumex crispus 30
    salicifolius 29
RUSH, BOG. 65
    IRIS. 66
    SCOURING. 20
    SPIKE 66
    WIRE. 66
SACRED DATURA 37
SAGE, BLACK 41
    PITCHER 41
SAGEBRUSH, CALIFORNIA 59
Salix Hindsiana 47
    lasiolepis 47
Salvia Columbariae. 41
    mellifera. 41
Sambucus mexicana. 54
SAN DIEGO PEA 47
SANDWORT 27
Sanicula crassicaulis 52
Saxifraga californica. 42
SAXIFRAGE, CALIFORNIA 42
Scandix pecten. 52
SCARLET BUGLER 38
SCARLET PIMPERNEL 30
Scirpus californicus 67
    microcarpus 66
SCOURING RUSH 20
Scrophularia californica 39
Scutellaria tuberosa 40
SEDGE 66
    UMBRELLA 66
SEDUM, MINATURE 42
Sedum spathulifolium 42
Selaginella Biglovii 20
SENECIO, CREEK 60
Senecio Brewerii. 60
    Douglasii 60
    vulgaris 60
SHEPHERD'S NEEDLE 52
SHOOTING STAR. 30
SIERRA MEADOWRUE 23
Silene gallica 27
SILVER HAIRGRASS 68
SNAKEROOT 52
SNAPDRAGON, BLUE 39
    SIERRA 39

SNAPDRAGON, VIOLET 39
SOAP PLANT 63
Solanum umbelliferum 37
Solidago californica 58
SPIKEMOSS 20
SPURGE 24
Stachys bullata 41
Stephanomeria virgata 62
STICKY POTENTILLA 43
STINGING NETTLE 48
STONECROP. 42
Streptanthus glandulosus 26
Stylomecon heterophylla 25
SYCAMORE, WESTERN 47
TARRAGON 59
TARWEED. 56-57
    CHILE 56
Tauschia Kelloggii 53
Thalictrum polycarpum 23
THELYPODIUM 25
Thelypodium lasiophyllum 25
THISTLE, BARNABY'S 61
    COBWEB. 61
    NAPA 61
    STAR 61
Thysanocarpus curvipes 26
TICKSEED 56
TIDY TIPS 56
Tillaea erecta. 42
TOBACCO, COYOTE. 37
    INDIAN. 37
TOCOLATE 61
TOOTHWORT 26
TORREY MELIC 68
TOYON 45
Trichostema lanatum. 40
    lanceolatum 40
TURKEY MULLEIN 24
TURKISH RUGGING. 28
TURK'S RUG. 28
Typha glauca 64
Urtica holosericea 48
UTAH JUNIPER. 22
VELAEA 53
VINEGAR WEED. 40
VIRGIN'S BOWER, WESTERN . . .23
Viola pedunculata 24
WALNUT, BLACK 48
WATERCRESS 26
WALLFLOWER, WESTERN 27
WHISPERING BELLS. 35
WILLOW, ARROYO. 48
    SANDBAR. 48
WINTER CRESS. 26
WIREWEED 57
WOODLAND STAR 43
Woodwardia fimbriata 21

WOOLLY BLUE-CURLS 40
WOOLLY INDIAN PAINTBRUSH 40
Wyethia helenoides. 55
YARROW, COMMON 59
         GOLDEN 57
YELLOW PANSY. 24
YERBA SANTA 35

YERBA SANTA, WOOLLY . . . 35-36
YUCCA .64
Yucca Whipplei 64
Zauschneria californica. 49
Zigadenus Fremontii. 63
       venenosus. 63